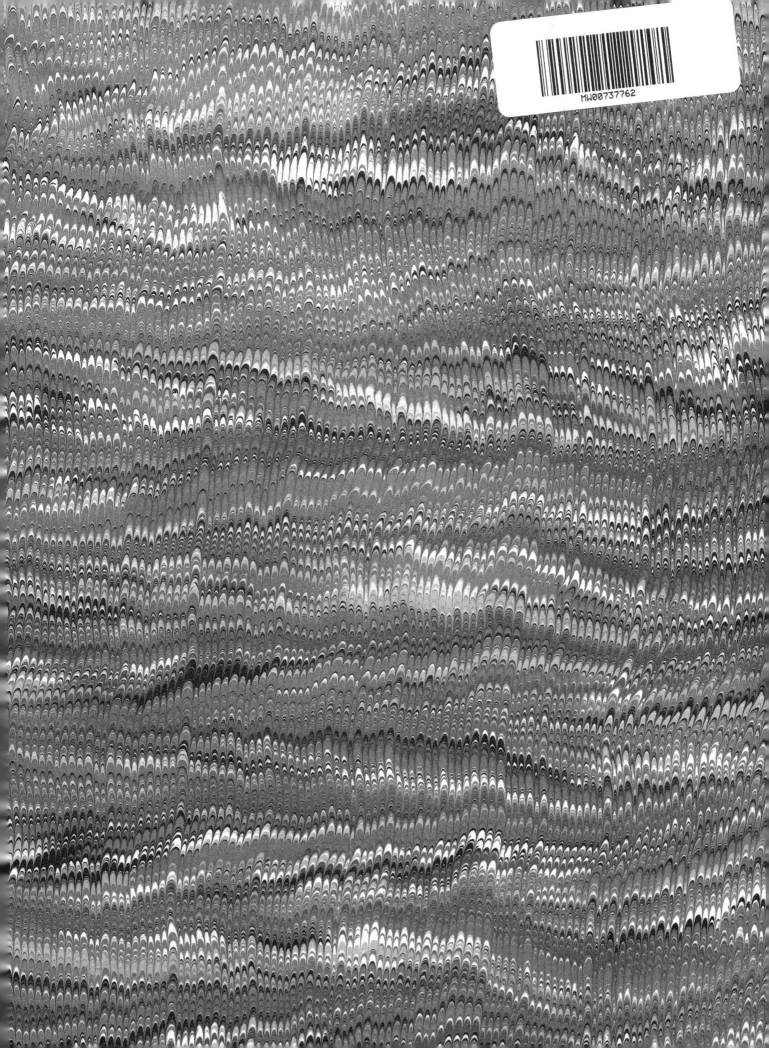

OCCUPIED JAPAN
FOR COLLECTORS

Florence Archambault

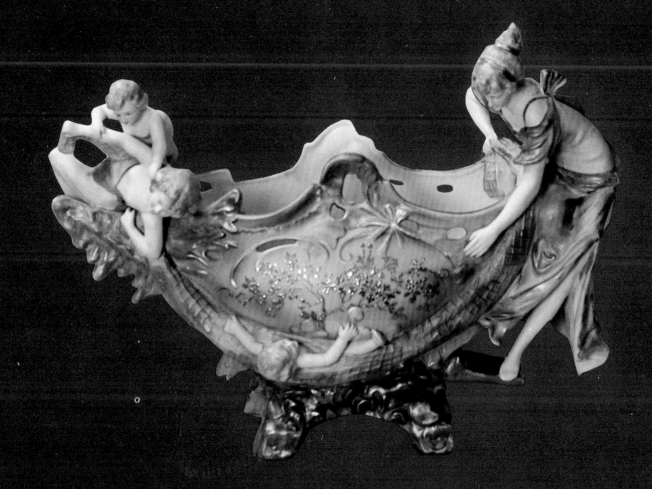

Schiffer Publishing Ltd

1469 Morstein Road, West Chester, Pennsylvania 19380

Title page photo:
This Art Nouveau bisque centerpiece is the pìece de resistence of my collection. A copy of a Royal Dux one, pictured in an auction ad in January, 1991, the differences are slight. They are mostly in the positioning of the figures. The classic Greek lady is hauling in a fishing net in which she has caught some cherubs. Meanwhile a cherub in the center, struggling to get out of the net, lies on his back with only his torso, two arms and a leg visible. It is 16" W. and 11¼" H. Mark #4 and G441.

Top row: A 10" dinner plate decorated with cherries. Mark #94. The floral decorated 10" dinner plate has a Noritake mark.
Bottom row: Cup and saucer is part of the set above decorated with cherries. Pot and creamer are from yet another dinner set and are marked FUJI China. The pot is 7½" H. and the creamer is 4" H. to the top of the handle.

Dedication

Dedicated to the memory of our son
Thomas Charles Archambault
July 2, 1957 — August 30, 1990
The Ultimate Collector

Published by Schiffer Publishing, Ltd.
1469 Morstein Road
West Chester, Pennsylvania 19380
Please write for a free catalog.
This book may be purchased from the publisher.
Please include $2.00 postage.
Try your bookstore first.

We are interested in hearing from authors with book ideas on related subjects.

Contents

A pair of double candelabras. The one on the right is missing a holder. They are 6″ H. on 5¾″ W. bases. A very nice quality with well defined fingers. The seated lady listens to the seated gentleman playing a flute. Decoration includes applied flowers and gold beading. Mark #4.

Acknowledgments

A book such as this is never the work of a single person. There are always others who contribute in some way or another and I would like to thank them.

Jim Garman...for his patience and sharing of expertise. Unless otherwise noted all photos are by Garman Photography of Portsmouth, R.I..

Margaret Bolbat, Art Gill, Josephine Stine and Wayne Walters...for contributing photos of their wonderful collections but especially to

Frank Travis...for sending me over one hundred photos of OJ marks. If I had had to draw them as I originally intended, this book would never have seen print.

Bob Gee of the inactive O.J. Collectors Club of Torrance, Ca.... for allowing me to utilize his club's newsletters.

Howard Singleton...for his research at the National Archives and his willingness to share it.

Kay O'Brien...for her assistance in proofreading all those pesky measurements.

Nancy Schiffer...for believing that the time was right for a book about OJ from a collector's viewpoint and for her patience with missed deadlines.

To the members of The OJ Club for their input into twelve years of newsletters and for patiently waiting for "the book" to be published.

And, most importantly, to my husband Tom...for all the hauling, packing, unpacking, aggravation, the doing of laundry, dishes and floors and for his love and support.

Thank you all.

A wonderful bisque centerpiece. The lady with her two angels seems to be awaiting someone's arrival. 7½" H.,8" W. and 5" deep. Mark #4. Margaret Bolbat collection.

Introduction

On September 7, 1945, the American flag was hoisted over the headquarters of General Douglas MacArthur in Tokyo and the formal occupation of Japan began. One of the first orders of business was to restore Japan's economy. While many of the manufactories had been damaged in the war, there were still enough operable ones remaining so that after a short time an attempt to resume manufacturing was underway.

Records on deposit at the National Archives in Washington, DC show that the first exports consisted of raw materials. At that time, foreign trade with occupied areas was conducted by the United States Commercial Company (USCC). The USCC was a government corporation established in 1942 within the Foreign Economic Administration for the purpose of purchasing, through foreign trade channels, materials and products deemed essential for the war effort. This served the dual purpose of insuring adequate supplies and preventing enemy acquisition. In October of 1945, the USCC was transferred to the Reconstruction Finance Corporation. Also in October of 1945, the War Department of the United States requested that the USCC handle exportation from Japan to the United States. The USCC sent a three-man mission to Japan late in 1945. The end result of this request by the War Department was a series of contracts between the USCC and the War Department covering trade with the occupied areas of Japan, Germany and Korea.

This contract was in effect from January 17, 1946 until December 31, 1947 covering all exports from Japan to the United States except textiles produced from Commodity Credit Corporation (CCC) cotton. On August 15, 1947, Japan was reopened for private trade with the admission of private business representatives into Japan for the resumption of foreign trade. After August 15, 1947 the USCC ceased exportation from Japan to the United States of all merchandise and products except raw silk and the 1947 green tea crop. All merchandise and products exported between August 14, 1947 and December 31, 1947 by the USCC had been contractually obligated prior to August 15th.

A 9" H. Geisha Girl doll in a 12" H. wooden box with paper labels. The doll, dressed in a brocade robe, stands on a wooden stand. The labels are pictured below. Margaret Bolbat collection.

Labels on bottom of box containing doll above tell us that it came from the Kyugetsu Dolls Store in Tokyo. Margaret Bolbat collection.

On December 31, 1947, all operations of the USCC were turned over to the Supreme Commander of the Allied Powers (SCAP). The only manufactured items brought into the United States during 1946 were Christmas tree lamps and sockets (sold from the dock in November, 1946) and several cases of samples of handicraft products that were exhibited to the trade in the showroom located at 292 Madison Avenue in New York City.

On February 20, 1947, SCAP issued a memorandum (SCAPIN-1535) to the Imperial Japanese Government on the subject of the marking of export articles stating that:

> 1. The Imperial Japanese Government is hereby directed to take immediate steps to insure that every article prepared for export after 15 days of receipt of this directive, the immediate container thereof and the outside package will be marked, stamped, branded or labeled in legible English with the words "Made in Occupied Japan."
>
> 2. All markings, stampings, branding or labeling shall be made in a conspicuous place and shall be as nearly indelible and permanent as the article will permit.

This makes the category of Occupied Japan collectibles a creation of the United States government. On August 14, 1949, SCAPIN-2061 was issued, again addressing the marking of export articles. This memoranda directed that all objects now be marked "Made in Occupied Japan", "Made in Japan", or "Japan." "Occupied Japan" was also used where there was limited space.

On April 25, 1952, the occupation of Japan ended and the military government's control ceased. While one era ended, a new one began. With the generous help of the United States a defeated nation had its economy restored, even made better than the economy enjoyed by the victor.

Although we know that many objects marked "Made in Japan" were imported to the United States during the occupation, OJ collectors only concern themselves with those that have the MIOJ or OJ marks, making these easy collectibles to identify.

The number and variety of exported objects defies documentation as records of exactly what was exported are scarce. The Japanese developed an ingenuity and ability to create for the American market goods that today command high prices at antique shows and flea markets.

Most people who think of the Japanese products of this period have a tendency to associate them with the inferior "knickknacks." While it is true that the dime-store market was targeted for much of this output, many superior items (particularly bisque ones) also were produced for finer gift shops and these are what advanced collectors attempt to find.

Besides the decorative pieces which flooded the market, utilitarian objects ranging from tools, ice-makers, sewing machines, and sports equipment to mustard plasters were made.

This book is designed to acquaint the reader with the wide scope of quality items produced during a short period (1945-1952), which can be found in today's market.

Values

I have attempted to place realistic values on these Occupied Japan items since I strongly feel that this is a difficult task. What a piece of OJ is worth to a buyer is dictated by many variabes—the foremost being the financial situation of the collector. Other factors include how long the piece has been sought to complete a set or a pair of figurines, the beauty and workmanship of the piece, and the rarity of the item.

Note

All items in this book, unless otherwise noted, are in the collection of the author.

I cannot stress enough the value of belonging to a collectors' club, regardless of what your area of collecting is. The benefits are tremendous. They increase your knowledge of your collectible, tell you what is out there to be found and what members are paying for items. They put you in touch with other collectors, and if they hold conventions the perks are even more wonderful. If you are interested in becoming a member of The OJ Club and receiving our newsletters, send a SASE to:

The OJ Club
% Florence Archambault
29 Freeborn
Newport, Rhode Island 02840 U.S.A.
for information.

Porcelain Singles

Porcelain figures are glazed and usually painted in vivid colors. They fall into many categories including the ones pictured here. Some of these singles could possibly have mates but many of them were made to stand on their own.

*Some single ladies, some of whom have become separated from their mates. **Top row:** Lady playing with a dog, 5½"H.; an 8" H. lady dressed in blue, Mark #52. This is of very good quality and the weight tells us that she probably was half of a pair of lamps. Her mate should be a copy of Gainsborough's* Blue Boy; *a white, brown and gold lady with a violin, 6½" H.; this lady with outstretched hands is 6" H.* **Middle row:** *Prim and proper lady holding purse, 4" H.; seated lady, 3¾" H.; bisque lady with a feather. She has the flat features shared by many of the cruder pieces, 6¾" H.; a 5" H. lady with basket.* **Bottom row:** *Skirt holding lady, 4½" H.; lady with basket and ruffled overskirt, 4¼" H.; street peddlar, 3¾" H. with blue MIOJ; another flat-featured lady holding a fan, 5" H.*

The ladies holding on to their hats do not have mates, neither do most of the dancing girls. The musicians may have, but I have never come across them.

Opposite page:
An assortment of some of the more commonly found porcelain Colonial male figurines looking for their mates. **Top row**: *6" to 6⅞" H.* **Second row**: *All 5¼" H. except for No. 5 which is 4¾" H.* **Third row**: *2¾" to 3¼" H.* **Bottom row**: *All are 4½" H. except for No. 3 which is 4" H. and bisque and No. 6 which is 3⅛" H.*

Dancing girls. **Top row**: *First lady is 6" H. Nos. 2, 3, and 4 are 6½" H. They have identical bases and are a set. They all seem to be having difficulty with their hats.* **Middle row**: *Nos. 1 and 4 are both 3¾" H.; No. 2 is 5⅜" H. and holds her skirt high; No. 3 rests a tambourine on her head; she is 5½" H.* **Bottom row**: *These tiny dancers measure from 2½" to 3" H. Nos. 1 and 6 have Mark #72.*

Four lady musicians. Nos. 1 and 4 playing the viola are made from the same mold but the right one feels lighter in weight and has more defined features; both are 3¼" H. The standing lady playing the violin is 3¼" H. while the lady playing the ukulele stands 3¾" H.

The ballerinas are just some of several collectors can find. It is difficult to find them in mint condition as the Japanese apparently had a problem perfecting the lace porcelain copied from the German originals and many are damaged. Some appear in poses that border on the awkward.

*Ballerinas are difficult to find without some kind of damage. The porcelainized skirts were extremely vulnerable to breakage. Many of these figurines strike awkward poses. **Top row**: These three are in excellent condition. No. 1 has an applied rose in her skirt, the second has Mark #94 in gold; the third is marked KOUWA, all are 3¾" high. **Bottom row**: This ballerina does not have a stiffened skirt and her green skirt is a bit rumpled. She is 6¼" H.*

The five seated musicians show the individual form that seemingly similar subjects can take. They are all very different from each other but accomplishing the same purpose...playing their instruments. Another opportunity for the collector to specialize.

*These five seated musicians are very different from each other. **Top row**: Two 3¾" H. figures, one plays a horn and the other a flute. They are white with gold decoration. Both sit on identical stools but one is marked MIOJ in red and the other in black. The skinny art deco musician playing a saxophone I am told is part of a set. He is 3⅝" H. **Bottom row**: Two concertina players wearing Greek fishermen hats are similiar in costume, stance and color but are from different molds. The left one is larger (4¾" H.) and is seated on a chair. He has a blue MIOJ mark. The other is 4½" H. and sits on a stool.*

The colorful ladies came in all sizes and shapes and dressed in all sorts of costumes. They are among the easier OJ figures to find.

*A half dozen ladies holding their skirts. **Top row**: A 4½" H. lady with gold highlights on her bodice and the front of her skirt. The next attractive lady has gold on the tie of her hat, 5¾" H. A 4½" H. lady is prepared for rain with her umbrella. **Bottom row**: This 4¾" H. lady is elevated by a rounded base. A young girl prepares to curtsy, 4¼" H. The final figure is 4½" H.*

*A bevy of porcelain ladies carrying baskets. **Top row**: Left to right: A 4¾" H. lady carrying a flower basket. Her bodice is outlined in gold. A 6" H. grey-haired woman carries two baskets —one of limes and one of lemons. She has gold highlights on her shoes, the ends of her shawl and around her neckline. A matte-finish servant girl carrying vegetables; 5¾" H. with gold lacing on her bodice. A genteel lady with a flower basket; 4⅛" H. **Bottom row**: A 4⅛" H. lady with wide-brim hat carries flowers. She has gold highlights around her bodice. Lady with flower basket has flower decals on her skirt. She stands 5⅛" H. A 5¾" H. blonde beauty carries a flower basket in each hand. A 5¼" H. woman with a tall hat holds a basket of flowers. Lady in three-tiered skirt stands 4½" H.*

The ladies and their dogs could have been made from molds that existed before the war. Their flapper-like clothing places them in that time period.

Two 6" H. flappers with their dogs. The lady with the greyhound is especially nice.

Ever mindful of the market they were targeting the Japanese came up with figurines which established a category called Americana. Our Northern neighbors provided an additional market so the Japanese came up with a Canadian Mounted Policeman. With the exception of the Uncle Sam figurine, most of these figures are not hard to find and make up the bulk of many OJ collectors' inventories.

There must be some of these bride and groom cake decorations packed away waiting to be unearthed. Porcelain and highly glazed, they are 4¾" H. This 4½" H. Northwest Mounted Policeman is ready for duty. The 4⅜" H. Uncle Sam also comes in a 6⅜" H. version. A hula dancer playing her ukulele is 4¼" H.

It's cowboy and Indian time! **Top row**: This 4½" H. cowboy has wide chaps; the girl is 4¼" H.; the pair of shelfsitters are 2¾" H. **Middle row**: The first pair of Indians are 4" H. The chief holds a rifle while the brave a tomahawk and some sort of shield. The Indian squaw is 5" H. The two cowgirls are 5" H. and 5¼" H.

Bottom row: A nice pair, 4" H. An Indian chief stands with folded arms while his sad-eyed dog leans against him and a bow-legged cowboy with his hand on his gun stands next to a vase; 4" H. on a 3" W. base.

Porcelain Pairs

The world of Occupied Japan collectibles is peopled with figurines depicting Colonial men and women, ethnic costumes, and copies of the European figures that were so popular as home decorations prior to the war. Many were fashioned for lamps, but quite a few were originally intended to stand on tables and mantels and behind the glass doors of curio cabinets.

Top row: Seated musicians are 6¼" H. with a black MIOJ circling Handpainted. A 9¼" H. Colonial pair with excellent detail; the man wears a curly wig. *Bottom row*: First pair are 5" H. and second pair is 6½" H. Both the man and woman hold a flower, and are wearing tricornered hats; the third pair are 5" H., the gentleman is marked only Japan in red while the lady has a red MIOJ.

A group of porcelain Colonial pairs. **Top row**: *Flower carrying pair are 7" H.; another pair carrying flowers is 9½" H.* **Bottom row**: *Seated pair, 3¾" H., he holds a violin, she a book; a pair of seated musicians, she with a ukulele and he with a horn, 3½" H.*

Three pair of figurines dressed in ethnic costumes. **Top row**: *A nicely glazed and decorated Dutch couple, 6¼" H.* **Bottom row**: *An 8" H. French country couple, possibly from Brittany. The gentleman in this 6½" H. Mexican pair has the inevitable sombrero, guitar and large mustache while his senorita holds flowers.*

These two figures comprise one of the larger porcelain pairs. They are 10¼" H. with Mark #39. She holds a rose while he serenades her with his mandolin. Frank Travis collection.

Top: This French pair are holding bunches of grapes; she in her apron, he with his lifted hand. The 6½" H. man has Mark #52 while the lady is simply marked with a red MIOJ. These were originally lamp decorations. They were purchased with the screws still intact on the bottom.
Bottom: A pair copied from the Dresden sweetmeat servers. The bunches of daisies form the dishes. 8¾" H. The lady is marked MIJ.

The challenge among collectors is to match up these pairs. Quite often you come across a very nice piece that you know must have had a mate at some time. The dilemma is whether or not to invest in the single and hope to find its mate or to pass it up. This is a personal decision that only the individual collector can make...but remember there are many stories of these singles being matched!

Here is a dancing couple decorated with cobalt blue and gold paint. Cobalt blue figures have become some of the more highly prized pieces collectors search for.

These two pair are from an identical mold but the difference in coloring makes them appear to be two entirely individual sets.

An elegant cobalt blue dancing couple clad in their ball attire are highlighted with gilt. Cobalt blue pieces are highly desirable additions to OJ collections. 8¾" H. with Mark #81.

This is a good example of how the same mold can be made into entirely different figurines simply by changing the color. They are 4¾" H. The men look very debonair in their tails and top hats. Both ladies have porcelainized lace collars and they are all marked with an S in a circle underneath what resembles an eyelash.

The cavalier and his lady are an illustration of the vivid coloring used in porcelain figures as opposed to the muted ones we find on the bisque pieces. The fact that the pieces are glazed also makes them more colorful.

The shepherd and shepherdess also come in bisque and are among some of the more desirable items that OJ collectors hope to find.

A 6¼" H. colorfully dressed cavalier and his lady. They both wear feathered hats and he has a gold sword on his left hip. Frank Travis collection.

This porcelain shepherd and shepherdess are among one of the more sought after pairs of figures by collectors. The set also comes in bisque. They each have a lamb on their shoulders. 12" H.

Porcelain Groups

Two figures on one base are referred to as doubles. These are some of the more common ones which were sold in the dime stores. A few may have had mates that were mirror images. Some of the better quality figurines are superior copies of the Meissen porcelains and command high prices. It is difficult to find three figures on one base.

*Some porcelain double Colonial figurines. These are good examples of the dimestore quality figures that many people associated with Japan and think of when they hear the words Made in Occupied Japan. **Top row**: The first is 3½" H.; No. 2 is a bisque couple with a lamb or dog and is 3¾" H. as is No. 3. **Middle row**: These three figures range from 3" to 3¾" H. **Bottom row**: Three that are about as a small as you can get. 2¼" to 2½" H.*

Since these two figurines have the same base we can assume that they were meant to be a pair. Indeed they were purchased together and have the same mark, a T over S. The left figure is 6¾" H. and the right is 6¼" H. They both sit on 4½" diameter bases which have square holes in the bottom leading one to assume that they once served as decorations on a pair of boudoir lamps. They greatly resemble Meissen porcelains. The left shows a pair of lovers in close proximity while in the right figure a lady plays her stringed instrument while the gentleman gives her his complete and undivided attention. A curly, wooly lamb lies at her feet.

Two lovers embrace tenderly in this 6¼" H. double figurine on a 4¼" W. base. A 17th century violinist is accompanied on the piano by his lady. His bow is missing but close inspection of his hand suggests he was never provided with one. This double is 6½" H. on a 5¾" W. base. Both pieces have Mark #52.

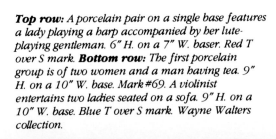

Top row: A porcelain pair on a single base features a lady playing a harp accompanied by her lute-playing gentleman. 6" H. on a 7" W. baser. Red T over S mark. **Bottom row:** The first porcelain group is of two women and a man having tea. 9" H. on a 10" W. base. Mark #69. A violinist entertains two ladies seated on a sofa. 9" H. on a 10" W. base. Blue T over S mark. Wayne Walters collection.

The Japanese cleverly copied the German coaches. The sulky with the man walking along side is an eyecatching piece.

Two porcelain horsedrawn coaches. **Top row**: *Commonly referred to as Cinderella's coach, it measures 6⅝" H. to the top of the coachman's head and is on an 8⅝" W. base.* **Bottom row**: *A gentleman wearing a top hat and carrying a cane walks along side a sulky. A carriage robe is thrown across the front and the lady cradles a bouquet of flowers in her arms. The piece measures 6¼" H. to the top of the lady's bonnet and is on an 8½" W. base. Both have Mark #69.*

This pair was purchased at a flea market from a lady who told me that during the Occupation years she and her husband had an import business in New York City. When they closed it down she kept some of the nicer OJ figurines and has just now brought them out to sell. She calls this pair Scarlett O'Hara and Rhett Butler but I'm not sure if those tight pants were in vogue during the Civil War.

A pair of figurines sometimes called the "Gone With the Wind" pair. They are not mirror images as the hands are positioned differently. They are 8½" H. on 5⅞" W. bases and were probably intended to be lamps. These were purchased mint from the original importer so we can assume that they never were made into lamps. Many figurines were imported here to be assembled into lamps and never were. Mark #52.

The porcelain couple, while romantic in their posture, look to me as though they are a bit uncomfortable.

A porcelain figure of a man cradling a girl across his lap. 4½" H. on a 6⅛" W. base. Frank Travis collection.

Porcelain Miscellany

What a wonderful word miscellany is! Here is an assortment of OJ porcelain pieces that defy categorizing, or are so few in number that they don't rate a chapter of their own. Nevertheless some of them are unusual and beautiful.

The figural inkwell is composed of a loving mother holding a frame around her child. As with any two-piece item we are fortunate that the pieces have not become separated.

A 5¼″ H. on a 5½″ W. base two-piece inkwell with a mother and child. The child is surrounded by an oval frame. The piece is highlighted with gilt. Mark #4.

The two-piece inkwell with its top removed. The top measures 3¾″ H. and the bottom 1½″ H. If you look closely you can see one of the child's feet in the bottom half.

A group of figurines all bear the Paulux mark. Because this mark has been found on other items along with a pottery mark, I think it is safe to assume that Paulux was the importer, not the manufacturer. The pieces which bear this mark are usually exceptional in quality.

This group of figurines are indicative of the quality of the pieces which are marked PAULUX. **Top row**: *A boy and his playful dog. 6" H. on a 4½" W. base. The rest of the set is pictured on page 86. A girl with three geese herds them along. She is carrying a staff and a bouquet of flowers. 5¼" on a 4½" W. base. Both these pieces have Mark #71.* **Bottom row**: *A seated pair. The lady is holding an envelope and reading the letter which came in it while her gentleman friend watches. 5¾" H. with Mark #70. The gentleman on bended knee appears to be proposing to the seated lady. His chair has four legs while hers is a solid piece of pottery with two legs visible in the rear. 5" H. on 5½" W. base with Mark #71.*

Representations of the many molded figures produced during the Occupation cover a variety of subjects. The Joan of Arc statue is particularly imposing.

A mirrored pair of porcelain girls with deer. 5⅛″ H. on a 4″ base. A full-figured porcelain Joan of Arc is dressed for battle. 8″ H. Josephine Stine collection.

A blacksmith plies his trade in this porcelain figurine marked Yamaka, 6″ H., 4″ W. base. A country girl with a basket on her back walks her cow, perhaps to market, 5½″ H., 6¼″ W. base. Josephine Stine collection.

A young girl is perched on two baskets, porcelain, Mark #4. The porcelain lady with the cart has the flattened features so predominant in many of the cruder OJ pieces. Both figures measure 4½″ x 4″. Josephine Stine collection.

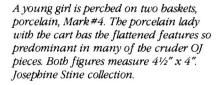

The Japanese employed a great deal of skill when they used the same theme, as in the four organ grinders, all just a little bit different.

The first and last organ grinders in this photo were cast from the same mold but their coloring makes them appear to be very different. Their monkeys sit on top of their hurdygurdys and hold up their cups for donations. 5½" H. The second and third Italian accordian players are similiar in stance but one does not have a monkey. The one without the monkey is 6½" H. and has mark #24. The other stands 5⅝" H.

Remember when the males of the family disposed of their used razor blades through a slot in the medicine cabinet? Well, if your cabinet didn't have that slot they could have used the barber inspired receptacle instead.

This 4" H. barber is a receptacle for used razor blades. Some had thought that it was a bank because of the slot in his head as some examples have surfaced without the word "BLADES" written on the back.

The back of the blade holder clearly states that this figure was intended for razor blade disposal.

These bookends function more as decoration. Their lack of weight prohibits standing too many books between them.

Two sets of bookends. One of the ladies is carrying an umbrella, 4-4¼" H. on a 2½" W. base. These came packed three to a box. Boy and girl in Dickens' costumes are also found painted in different colors, 4" H. on a 2¼" W. base. Both sets are highlighted in gold.

The Japanese were advanced in the manufacture of the lady head vases that are now a popular collectible. These are a bit smaller than the American ones made recently, but have just as much appeal.

Five of these highly glazed porcelain lady heads are part of a set. As usual, in this crazy collectible, who knows how many make up this set. They are 3 to 3¼" H. The sixth bisque figure has an opening in the top of her head. She seems to have been fashioned from a similiar mold as the others.

Some porcelain powder jars were decorated with the familiar rose decals found on many of the ceramics made in Japan, both before and after the war.

A two-piece hobo resting on a bench has a number of stamps on it, including the importer's logo.

An interesting large (11″ high) pottery water pump might have served as a planter. The 3″ wide bucket could have held a small pot.

This lovely porcelain powder jar would make an elegant addition to milady's dressing table. The bottom is 3¾″ in diameter and when the top is on the piece is 5¼″ H. Mark #94 in gold plus a red MIOJ.

A two piece porcelain hobo on a park bench is 3¾″ H. to the top of his hat x 4″ W. Also marked with the name of the importer, Pioneer Mdse. Co., N.Y. The owner has two sets of this figurine. The hobo in one set is marked in black and in the other in red. Frank Travis collection.

The bottom of the bench above shows both a red and black Pioneer Mds. Co. logo, a red MIOJ and a black MIJ. Frank Travis collection.

This 11″ brown pottery water pump is accompanied by a 2¾″ H. bucket. It is embossed MIOJ. Frank Travis collection.

Bisque Angels and Cherubs

The number of figurines made of bisque featuring angels and cherubs is incredible. Bisque is a white, unglazed porcelain, which was fired once and has no glaze or a very thin one, usually painted in soft, pastel shades. While some authors have mistakenly written that OJ bisque does not rival the European originals it was copied from; some of the pieces pictured in these chapters show very high quality. However, not all bisque was finely done. Some molds produced statutes with blunted surfaces.

Many of these pieces feature a putto (a very young boy, somewhat like a wingless cherub or cupid). This was a popular subject used for decoration during the Italian Renaissance.

Some statues do have wings. These four provide a good example of how it is possible to add to an incomplete set. For a number of years the owner of three of them advertised for one he called Fall. One day in a local antique shop I found one marked Autumn. Sure enough, it was the one he needed to complete his set. When he decided to sell his collection, he offered them to me first since I had helped him find the missing link.

This bisque piece, although pleasing to the eye, is an example of the crude features which appeared on some of the faces of some of the figurines. Just because the figurine is bisque, it does not follow that it is a valuable piece. The mold for this piece does not clearly define the cherub's features. 3¼″ H. and 5″ W. Frank Travis collection.

A set of four 7¼″ H. bisque cherubs representing the four seasons. SPRING holds a basket of flowers; SUMMER, a sheaf of grain; AUTUMN, a branch of bittersweet; WINTER is clothed in a scarf.

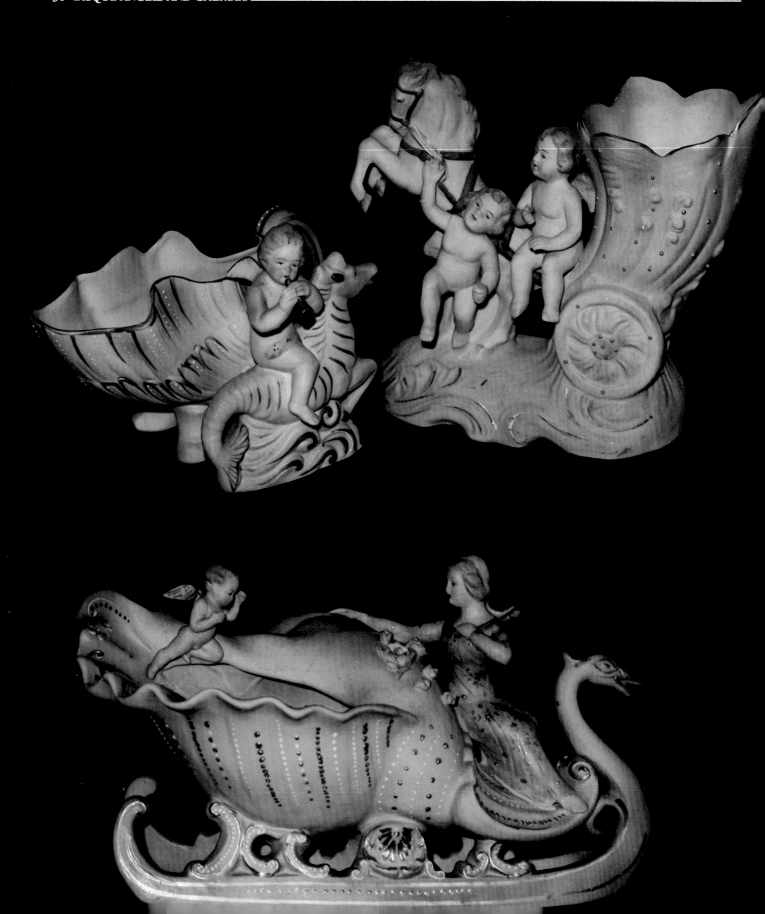

A pair of bisque angel busts, 2¾" H. One holds a lyre and the other a scroll. Flower detail inside wings. Marked MIOJ Lamore China #432. A bisque angel sits on a colorful glazed butterfly and tree stump, 3½" H.

A bisque angel pulls a cart decorated with large roses, 5" H. and 7¾" W. Mark #62. Margaret Bolbat collection.

A gold beaded bisque centerpiece with two angels and two doves, 7" H., 9" W., 4½" deep with Mark #4. Margaret Bolbat collection.

Opposite page top:
Two bisque centerpieces. The left measures 5⅛" H. x 7" W. An angel blows a horn while astride a stylized seahorse in front of a shell bowl. The right one measures 7¼" H. x 6¾" W. Two angels sit in front of a rearing horse pulling a chariot. Frank Travis collection.

Opposite page bottom:
A magnificent bisque sleigh pulled by the classic serpent has as its passenger a girl clad in Greek costume and a small winged cherub. Its measurements of 7" H. and 12" W. make it an impressive piece. Mark #4. Wayne Walters collection.

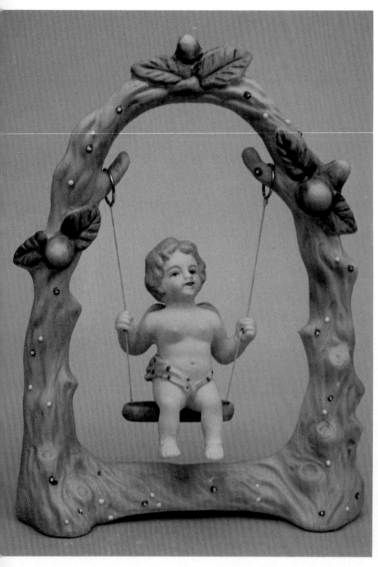

A bisque cherub enjoys his swing from this tree bough, 7" H. and 5¼" W. Margaret Bolbat collection.

A pair of 6½" H. bisque angel artists seated on tree stumps at their easels painting pictures of castles. Although not identical, the left-handed painter makes them a mirror image. Mark #9 6297. Superb detail.

These ducks are very much interested in what this nude cherub holds in his hands, 4" x 5", Mark #69 in red. The 5"x 3" bisque box with reclining nude is marked Hal-Sey Fifth Ave. Josephine Stine collection.

Opposite page:
Top row: *Nos. 1 and 3 are 6¾" H. while the 6½" H. cherub with the old fashioned shoe is marked Hand Painted Andrea.* **Bottom row:** *These two figurines playing musical instruments are both 7" H. Margaret Bolbat collection.*

Two seated bisque boys on a single base are marked Hal-Sey Fifth Ave. They measure 3¾" x 5½". The bisque vase with the three cherubs is 5" x 4½". Josephine Stine collection.

Top: A bisque angel with wings sits on three cornucopias decorated with gold beads, 7" H. **Bottom:** A 5" H.bisque angel astride a fish vase; a 6" H. bisque angel playing drum; a 5½" H. bisque angel playing concertina with a cornucopia decorated in gold beading.

A 5" H. angel pushes a sleigh on a 6¼" W. base, Mark #5 all in red. A pair of bisque cherubs, one leading a band and the other playing a stringed instrument, 4½" H. on a 5¼" W. base, Marked Hal-sey Fifth Ave. L & M. A bisque angel seated on a carriage pulled by an Egyptian-like figure, 5¾" H. on 4¾" W. base.

Top row: A bisque lady perches on the edge of a shell, the piece is 8" H. and 8⅛" W. Mark #4. A cherub holds the head of a horse pulling a lovely decorated chariot, 6¼" H. and 9½" long, Mark #7. **Bottom row**: An impressive bisque swan sleigh with a lady and cherub, 6⅛" H. and 8¾" long. Mark #4. The lady with the jug spills water onto the ground while her companion stares off into the distance, 5½" H., 6¾" long, Mark #71. Margaret Bolbat collection.

Bisque Groups

Some of the most avidly sought after OJ are the pieces which have more than one figure on them. We have seen many of these in the preceding chapter featuring angels and cherubs. This group is peopled with humans and are reproductions of the finely crafted Meissen and Dresden that inspired them.

A bisque gentleman serenades his lady. She listens intently as she pats the lamb in her lap. Finely detailed with separate fingers on both figures. 6½" H. on a 6¾" W. base.

Left to right: A bisque pair of dancers in country costumes are 10" H. on a 5½" W. base. This figurine also comes in porcelain. A bisque pair dressed in ball costume are 8" H. on a 6" W. base. The man on his knees earnestly pleads his case with the lady with the angel on her shoulder. 7" H. on an 8" W. base. All have Mark #4. Wayne Walters collection.

One of the more popular figures is what some collectors call Cinderella's coach. This piece comes with either two or four horses. There is always a coachman sitting on the box holding the reins, a lady alighting, and a gentleman either offering her a hand or bowing from the waist. Many have the rectangular opening on the bottom which tells us that they were made for lamp bases. It is difficult to tell if the lamps were dismantled or if they were sold originally as figurines.

Three bisque coaches. **Top row**: *The coach with two horses measures 6" H. x 8" W. and has Mark #52.* **Middle left**: *A coach with four horses is 6" H. and 9" W. Mark #4.* **Bottom right**: *A large bisque coach also has four stalwart horses and the everpresent gentleman helping his lady to alight. 8" H. x 13½" W. Wayne Walters collection.*

A 5¼" H. bisque coach with two horses on a 7" W. base. Marked TOKAI MIOJ. Another possible lamp figurine which was either never assembled as a lamp or was taken apart for the figurine.

One planter is adorned with two children dressed in 17th-century clothing playing on a seesaw or teeterboard. The lady and two dogs is another statue done with care and highly crafted execution.

A most unusual group of bisque boys, German in appearance, are playing in a band. Pieces with more than three figures on them are rare.

An unusual bisque four-figured children's band on one base. The left figure carries a bass fiddle on his back. The piece is 5½" H. on a 7½" W. base. Frank Travis collection.

Two bisque children in 17th century costume perched on a teeter board. As was the custom of the day they are dressed as miniature adults. 8¾" H. x 10½" W. Mark #107. Margaret Bolbat collection.

A nicely crafted Art Deco bisque lady with two dogs resembling wolfhounds. It is 6½" H. and 7¼" W. Frank Travis collection.

Bisque Pairs

The majority of bisque pairs are reproductions of the European 17th-century attired men and women, but once in a while along comes something out of the ordinary. For example, a 17½" high knight and his lady show a degree of detail that rivals any of the European statuettes. They are extremely heavy and their rectangular opening on the bottom tells us that they were another pair intended to serve as lamp decorations. What a magnificent pair of lamps they must have made! They have also been found in porcelain mounted on heavy metal bases.

The backs of the 17½" H. Knight and his lady in photo below are as interesting as the fronts. He stands against a pillar and his sword is decorated with gold. The detail and the gold beading in this pair are extraordinary. A real find!

This is one of the most spectacular pairs of Occupied Japan I have ever seen. This 17½" H. Knight and his lady are standing on 5½" x 6" bases and have Mark #81. There is much gold decoration and she holds a gold cup above her head. They appear to have served as lamp bases.

Other large pairs were destined for lamp bases. However, standing on their own, they make admirable additions to our collections and command very high prices. Even slightly smaller pairs are just as impressive.

Large 15" H. bisque couple. Mark #7 and Nos. 6265 A & B. The man plays a guitar while the lady accompanies him with a pair of castanets. Art Gill collection.

A bisque pair dressed in their Sunday best, she stands 16½" H. and he stands 17½" H. Their garments are highly decorated with gold. Mark #107. Margaret Bolbat collection.

An 11¾" H. bisque couple dressed in 17th century French garb hold doves. Josephine Stine collection.

Two bisque couples and a porcelain lady. First couple is 11½" H., marked Hal-Sey Fifth Ave. Second couple is 13" H. Josephine Stine collection.

An unusual pair are the two blackamoors. They are both playing musical instruments. A happy standing baby and a scowling seated baby are a pair of nice figures. I wonder if there is any significance to the fact that the crying baby is wearing the pink diaper?

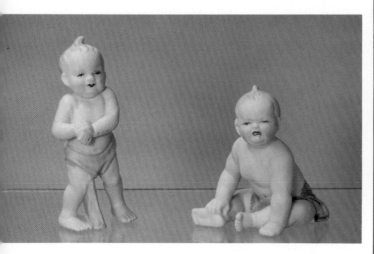

This pair of bisque babies were purchased separately, showing that it is possible to sometimes match up pairs. It was, however, not until I got the standing one home that I realized they were a pair. The standing baby is 5¾" H. while the crying baby is 4½" H.

A pair of 6¼" H. Bisque Blackamoor musicians. One beats a drum with his hand while the other uses a drumstick. Mark #28. Frank Travis collection.

Other figurines were inspired by royalty. The king and queen in the first pair remind us of the descendents of Queen Victoria who ruled Europe in the early 20th century. The second pair of bisque busts are French in appearance, and are another pair we can call "nicely done."

I always thought that this 6" H. bisque pair were Nicholas and Alexandra, Czar and Czarina of Russia during the 1915 revolution, but closer scrutiny shows the initial "J" on her back and "H" on his. Mark #71. The bisque French busts are of the Napoleonic period. She is 6⅞" H. and he is 6⅝" H. Nice detail.

"Spectacular" is the only word which can describe the dandy and his lady. They served as lamp bases but are just as attractive as figurines.

This exceptional bisque pair were originally lamp bases. The man is 14" H. and the lady is 13½" H. Mark #52. They are exceptional, not only for their height, but for the craftsmanship exhibited in the molds and the delicacy of the coloring. Wayne Walters collection.

The remaining examples, a group of children, men and women in various dress and poses, contradict the assumption that the output of the Japanese potteries during the Occupation was of a crude nature and of no value. They add credibility to our collectible.

Bisque 6" W. man and woman vases dressed in French costume. He wears a Napoleonic hat and stands 7½" H., she is 7" H. Mark #71. Margaret Bolbat collection.

Two bisque pair, both marked Hadson. The first pair are hunters shown with their dogs, 6¼" H. The lady in the second pair holds an umbrella while her companion holds what appears to be a cane, 6¾" H. Josephine Stine collection.

Two pair of delightful bisque children. First pair with roses on fence have Mark #4. Second pair are marked MIOJ. Both pair are 9¼" H. Josephine Stine collection.

Top row: *7⅝" H. bisque man and 7⅜" H. bisque woman. She appears to be carrying a tambourine. The next bisque pair are barefoot. She carries a basket of fruit and he has a glass in his right hand and his hat in his left, 5⅝" H.* **Bottom row**: *A bisque Scotch lassie and laddie in authentic costume, 4½" H. with M inside a C MIOJ. A bisque planter with a French couple carrying wreaths of flowers, 5½" H. x 4¼" W. x 3¾" deep. Mark #71.*

A bisque French country couple. She carries a bird cage while the bird perches on her left hand. Mark #107. 7½" H.

A 10" H. typical Colonial bisque couple of very nice quality highlighted with gold.

An 8" high pair of bisque children with Mark #107. Leaning against a beehive he holds a bird in the palm of his left hand and a sheaf of wheat in his right while she carries a basket of grapes and other fruit.

And More Bisque

It may be that big is not always beautiful, but the 18" H. swashbuckling cavalier certainly refutes that old cliche. Can you imagine what his mate looks like! Another outstanding piece is the lady with her puffed sleeves and hair piled high upon her head.

The Japanese sometimes paid a great deal of attention to detail. Note the tumbled iceskater wearing a garter on her left leg!

An 18" H. swashbuckling Cavalier in bisque. We can only imagine what his lady looks like. There is gold and white beading in the flowers. He carries a shoulder bag and wears cuffed boots and a plumed hat. Mark #4.

A marvelous 9¾" H. bust of an elaborately gowned and coiffured lady. Mark #7. Margaret Bolbat collection.

Among OJ collectors this bisque figurine has come to be known as the "tumbled ice skater". 4" H. and 5½" long. Mark #7. Margaret Bolbat collection.

The single ladies range in size from 10″ to 13″ inches in height. They all have mates somewhere and if matched up with them would be imposing pairs.

The smaller figurines are also missing their mates. One of the challenges in collecting OJ (or anything else that comes in pairs) is matching up the singles in your collection. (I always say I'm never going to buy another single...until one turns up that is either priced right or is so beautiful that I can't refuse it.) It can be done...but sometimes matching takes a lot of patience and luck.

Two bisque ladies. The first carries a basket of flowers, wears a broad brimmed hat, and holds up her skirt. She is 11¾″ H. Mark #107. The second lady, holding her skirt, is 13″ H. and has both Mark #62 and the PAULUX stamp. Margaret Bolbat collection.

A 10″ H. bisque lady with jug on a 6½″ W. base at a floral decorated well. She has a mate, also standing at a well. An 11½″ H. pensive bisque lady stands by a fence with a sheaf of grain and a jug on her left hip.

A 7⅜″ H. bisque Colonial man carrying a bouquet of flowers; a 9½″ H. bisque lady with her hands over her ears, perhaps she doesn't like her neighbor's music, Mark #71; he wears a cape and plays the lute, 8″ H.

Bisque 6" H. cavalier. The 8" H. lady in the bisque pair has just poured a drink for the gentleman. Mark #71. Josephine Stine collection.

The three monkeys, although illegibly marked, represent the See No Evil, Hear No Evil, Speak No Evil set. They are blessed with faces only a mother could love. Round holes in their backs suggest that they could be hung on the wall.

Three unusual bisque monkeys. Obviously designed to represent See No Evil, Hear No Evil, Speak No Evil, they are marked across their backs in an illegible script. The first words on each are definitely see, hear and talk, but the second (which is the same on all) appears to be zoll? They are 5½" long from their heads to their tails.

The Madonnas alert us that church bazaars are a good place to search for OJ. The Lamore China ones are of a superior quality. The rosary beads, however, are not of the best workmanship. The two-figured statue, although bisque, again points up that some were poorly molded. Also made for the American trade were Nativity scenes. When found, most of them are missing the Christ Child or other figures. Very rarely is a set found intact. A bisque Infant of Prague and Madonna planter have also been found.

Centerpieces are some of the better pieces made for the gift shop trade. Many are profusely highlighted with gold decoration.

A 7" H. bisque man and sleigh sits on a 9¼" W. and 3¾" deep footed base. Mark #81. Margaret Bolbat collection.

*A collection of Madonnas. **Top row**: A 7" H. bisque Madonna bust on a rose decorated base, marked Lamore China in cursive writing, 433 MIOJ, all in black. A similiar Madonna, 5¼" H. without the base, marked Lamore China 619 in red cursive writing, MIOJ in black. An 8½" H. bisque full-figured Madonna with Christ Child, marked Lamore China 542 in script and MIOJ, all on red. These are three variations of the same mark. **Bottom row**: A 7⅜" H. porcelain praying Madonna, Mark #28. A 6" H. bisque Madonna with praying child on a 3⅜" W. base. A pair of simulated pearl and gold chain Rosary beads stamped MIOJ on front of thin metal cross, can be read from back. The 1" H. cross on a 13" long chain is from the collection of Jessie Lange.*

The remaining figures are all good examples of the bisque that was produced during that short period (1947-1952). They are out there...you just have to persevere and hope that the price is right.

Top row: A 7" H. bisque Oriental couple carrying flowers; marked ORION. *Bottom row*: Bisque swan with applied roses and highlighted with gold, 3½" H. and 5" W. Marked in red LAMORE CHINA ENTIRELY HAND MADE G.Z.L. USA MADE IN OCCUPIED JAPAN. A 3½" H. bisque bird with open beak, Mark #94.

Top: Bisque lady decorated with lily pads and two swans. 6¾" H. on a 5¾" W. base, Jessie Lange collection. *Bottom*: A four-figure bisque group with two ladies and two angels. The lady with the grapes is looking at her reflection in a gold shell mirror; 7⅞" H. with a T over S mark. Multi-figured pieces are scarce and avidly sought after. A 7⅞" H. bisque ice skater has gold beading on her skating outfit.

Top row: Bisque vase with figure of 7" H. lady, 3½" W. base, Mark #69 in red; a 7½" H. girl with uplifted arm wearing a kerchief, Mark #69 in black. *Bottom row*: Bisque girl with an umbrella and picnic basket encounters a deer. 5¼" H. on a 4¼" W. base. Mark #69 in red. This figure was also made in porcelain. A pair of bisque Dutch children vases, 6¾" H. on 4" W. bases, Mark #4.

Oriental Figurines

It should not surprise us that the Japanese included among the many figurines they produced for the American trade some which represented their own people. These came in bisque and in porcelain. They are clad in both peasant and royal costume and engaged in various activities and poses.

Two 6¼" H. pair of bisque Oriental statues. The lady on the left carries a flower. Her companion standing on one leg carries a basket of flowers. The lady on the right holds a basket of flowers while her companion has a musical instrument. Mark #28. Josephine Stine collection.

Two pair of 8" H. porcelain Oriental men and women. The first pair are another variation on the two pictured on page 54. The second pair are striking in their yellow and black costumes. She holds a gold bottle while he strums a mandolin. Josephine Stine collection.

Although made from the same molds, the decoration on two couples causes them to seem very different from each other. Some collectors call the basket the man is carrying a suitcase and others (because he also holds a paint brush) call it a paint box.

These four Oriental heads make up two pair. The center two are a match as are the two outside ones. They feature very definite Oriental-type eyes.

These two pair of Orientals are a good illustration of how figurines made from the same mold can be made to look entirely different by a change in their decoration. They both stand 8½" H. The simplicity of the left pair is highlighted by the use of the wonderful bluegreen paint. The opulence of the second pair is enhanced by the use of a dragon motif and gold highlights.

Two pair of porcelain Oriental busts. They are 6⅛" H. Nos. 1 and 4 are mates as are the center pair. They all wear very Japanese-looking headdresses. Josephine Stine collection.

The remaining photos are a selection of the many Oriental figurines which can be collected today.

Top row: *The porcelain Oriental pair are 7½" H. and have Mark #62 and 1017 embossed on both bottoms. She has a fan and he holds a sword. A 6" H. girl stands next to a jug and holds a fan.*
Bottom row: *Five Oriental musicians play a variety of instruments. 4½" H.*

Top row: *A pair of porcelain Siamese dancers. The lady is 7½" H. and the man is 7¾" H. They are both marked with a R in a circle MIOJ similiar to Mark #104 but the lady in red and the man in blue. A bisque Siamese sword dancer measures 8⅜" H. Mark #107.* **Middle row**: *A 4" H. pair of Orientals each hold musical instruments. A 3" H. man has his hands in his kimono sleeves. The 3¼" H. pair are typically oriental.* **Bottom row**: *A pair of delightful Oriental children with animals. 3¾" H. They both carry closed umbrellas. The boy is accompanied by a dog and two puppies and the girl by a mother rabbit and her two babies.*

Top row: *An oriental porcelain man with two ladies. Perhaps Siamese? The two on the left are a pair while the one on the right is made from the same mold but decorated differently. 6¾" H.*
Middle row: *A seated man serves as an incense burner. 4⅜" H. This rickshaw with its passenger stands 4½" H. on a 3⅝" W. base.*

Bottom row: *A 10" H. figure is dressed in the clothing of the upperclass. The kissing pair are 3¼" H. on a 3¾" W. base. The girl is marked with a red R in a circle MIOJ similiar to Mark #104. The boy is simply marked MIOJ.*

A group of Oriental figures. **Top row:** *A 7" H. girl with fan; mirrored pair, two figures on one base, 7½" H.; bearded elder with mandolin, 5" H.; a 5" H. Geisha girl with an umbrella.* **Middle row:** *A pair of 4¼" H. children musicians with wonderful facial details; two figured man and woman musicians, 5½" H.; cavorting man and woman with flowers, 6" H.* **Bottom row:** *A pair of children, girl with baskets, boy with coolie hats, 5" H. with Ugaco mark in black, boy has an opening in back; elderly grey-haired grandmother with cane, 4½" H.; musical children on one base, 4" H.*

The Japanese made some amazing copies of the well European pottery. Some of the more spectacular are their Royal Dux copies. The Bisque and porcelain centerpieces are probably some of the best. They are exquisitely done and, if the mark were removed, could pass as the original.

This piece will hold water for flowers. A copy of what looks like a Royal Dux centerpiece. Dimensions approximately 12 inches wide.

The Royal Doulton factory furnished prototypes for many OJ pieces. The Japanese had no compunction in copying their Toby mugs or the Balloon Man and Woman. Even though they are done a little crudely, there is no doubt about their origin. The Japanese bulldogs, too, are just as nicely glazed as the many Royal Doulton animal figurines.

Jester Toby mug is a faithful copy of its Royal Doulton original, a favorite among collectors. 4½" H. x 5½" W. Mark #97. Art Gill collection.

Copies of the Royal Doulton Balloon Man and Woman. They are 3½" H. and a little less finely crafted than the originals.

Two Royal Doulton-like sad looking bulldogs. 3¾" H. x 5" W. Art Gill collection.

Other British potters were also copied. Most of the Wedgwood copies were inferior, although some were passable. Genuine Wedgwood, however, is fine-grained stoneware and velvety to the touch, which these are not. The Staffordshire dogs are presentable copies.

These Staffordshire dogs are 3¾" H. Mark #96. They are sand-finished like their British counterparts.

A variety of Wedgwood copies. The vases range in size from 2" to 3¾". Note the cowboy on the front of the center piece. An unlikely subject for Wedgwood! Two of the vases with spouts picture children which resemble the decoration on the Mary Gregory glass that is so popular with collectors. The rest have the more classical English designs. Frank Travis collection.

The Meissen and Dresden factories of Austria and Germany did not escape the imitative abilities of the Japanese potters, either. The children busts are among the finest I have ever come across. Each strand of hair on the larger ones is individually painted on. They are absolutely breathtaking! Other Meissen and Dresden copies also have finely defined features.

These two pair of children busts are faithful reproductions of their European counterparts. The small ones are 5" H. The left child has blue eyes while the right has brown. Both have applied flowers. The larger pair measures 7½" H. and has finely painted strands of hair. The girl's hair is tied into two ponytails with ribbons and both busts have applied flowers at the bodice. All four of these children have Mark #4.

Top row: *A 6⅜" H. seated lady holds a book while her 6½" H. mate grasps a stringed instrument; the four-figured center group is 8" H., 5⅛" W. and 3¾" deep and is marked handpainted, T over S, MIOJ, Ardalt 6055 U.* ***Bottom row***: *Seated 6⅛" H. gentleman listens to his lady playing her instrument, she is 6" H.; center piece has a lady seated at a piano; 5½" H., 5¼" W. and 3¾" deep. Both are marked Handpainted T over S MIOJ. Margaret Bolbat collection.*

The Royal Bayreuth look-a-likes are apt to fool even the most astute until they are turned over. I am forever turning over pieces to discover that they are authentic Royal Bayreuth, when I had hoped that they were OJ.

A wonderful collection of red tomato pieces in the Royal Bayreuth tradition with strawberries and red peppers thrown in for good measure. **Top row**: Three piece tea set. The pot is 4" H. to the tip of the spout, sugar is 3" H. to stem and the creamer is 2½" H. to its spout. **Middle row**: A tomato salt and pepper on 5" W. tray,; a 7" W. leaf dish which could be a tray minus its condiment set; strawberry salt and pepper set on a 4½" triangular tray with flower decoration and a yellow handle. **Bottom row**: A larger 3¼" H. creamer and sugar. Both the red peppers and tomato shakers are on similiar trays. Except for the shakers, which are marked Japan, all pieces are marked with the same black MIOJ.

Capo-Di-Monte porcelain was also cleverly copied with the applied florals and encrusted decoration in high relief that is characteristic of the ware. The variety of the Delft-like copies of Bing and Grondahl are also collectible. There is a difference of opinion among collectors about whether or not pieces should be termed Delft if they have traces of pink in them. I feel those touches of color make them more attractive.

Cherubs cavort on this centerpiece fashioned in the style of Capo-Di-Monte. The opening measures 7" and it is 5½" H. Mark #89. The bottom centerpiece of an angel holding a bowl with applied red berries is a copy of some of the Dresden porcelains. It is 6" H. on a 5½" W. base.

Delft porcelain figures. **Top row**: *The man in this 7" pair is called "Blue Boy" by many collectors. He reminds one of Gainsborough's painting; a 3¾" H. windmill with a Delft design and movable blade; a 5" H. fisherman and his wife, she carries a basket on her left hip and he carries a net over his shoulder.* **Middle row**: *A 5" H. lady with tambourine; a 5"H. lady with umbrella; a 6½" H. lady in ball gown with fan and opening in back; a 5½" H. lady holding skirt and hat; a 5½" H. lady holding tambourine behind head.* **Bottom row**: *First two ladies appear to be the same but closer scrutiny reveals slight variations, one is thinner than the other and the pose is different, 5½" and 5¼" H.; a 5¼" H. dancing lady holding skirt; the 5¼" H. ladies with plumed hats seem alike but again we see subtle differences. All these pieces are marked with a deep Delft blue MIOJ.*

Hokutosha

The HOKUTOSHA mark is found most often on Imari style pieces. The older Japanese porcelain called Imari was not named for a pottery but rather for the northern trading port of Imari. It has come to signify those pieces with an overglaze enamel decoration which includes red, gold, blue and other enamel colors. Most of the pieces marked MIOJ have deep blue, red and orange overglaze with a profusion of gold decoration.

These pieces are as elegant as their antique ancestors and they offer an excellent opportunity to upgrade one's collection.

The mark consists of a decal (see Mark #32) under the glaze on the bottom of the piece. The Hokutosha pottery made many decorative items including cigarette boxes, toothpicks, dishes, cups and saucers, and bowls. The popularity and beauty of this Imari ware is sending the prices up as collectors realize its importance.

This Imari-type cigarette box measures 2¾" x 4" x 1 5/6". Mark #32. Margaret Bolbat collection.

*A selection of Imari designed pieces all bearing the HOKUTOSHA mark. Mark #32. **Top row**: The coal scuttle stands 2⅞" H. on a 4¼" W. tray; the handled basket is 4" H.; the slipper measures 2⅝" H. on a tray that is 4¾" x 3¼". **Bottom row**: A 2¼" H. cigarette lighter sits on a tray that is 5⅜" x 3½"; the urn is 3⅛" x 1¾" x 1¾"; the salt and pepper shakers measure 2¾" H. and 3¾" H. Margaret Bolbat collection.*

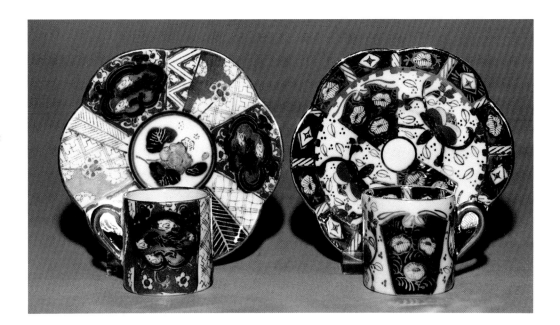

Two Imari-type cups and saucers. Both saucers are 3⅛" in diameter and the cups are 1¼" H. Mark #32. Margaret Bolbat collection.

Four cups and saucers, Imari pattern, ranging from 1½" H. to 2" H. The box measures 2¾" x 4" x 1⅝"; the bowl is 7" W. and stands 2⅝" H. while the urn is 4" H. and 4¼" W. All have Mark #32. Margaret Bolbat collection.

A decorative Imari-type bowl with the HOKUTOSHA mark; 9½" long and 9" W. Margaret Bolbat collection.

Two charming girls bearing the HOKUTOSHA mark. The one wearing the black hat is labeled WALES and stands 5⅜" H. The other is marked ENGLAND and is 5¼" H. Both of these figurines are also marked Bone China. Margaret Bolbat collection.

The HOKUTOSHA mark is also found on some very fine figurines, including exquisite bone china figures wearing the costumes of Wales and England. There is speculation that there may be more, perhaps representing other parts of Great Britain, but none have come to light so far.

Excellent copies of the German Hummels also bear this mark. A mini cup and saucer also departs from the Imari ware and its applied decoration of blue flowers are a delight to the eye, causing the OJ collector to believe that this mark is to be found only on high quality pieces.

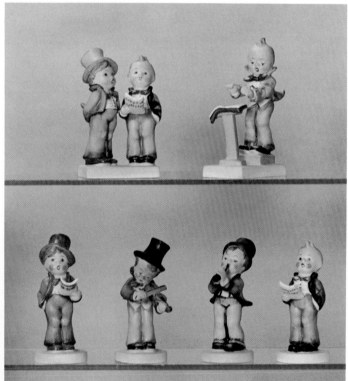

An unusual mini cup and saucer with applied blue flowers. Note the decoration is also on the bottom of the saucer. Mark #32. Margaret Bolbat collection.

This set of porcelain musicians and singers are all marked with the HOKUTOSHA mark and are of exceptional quality. They stand 5¼" H. Five of them are exact reproductions of their Hummel counterparts. No. 1 on the top shelf is a copy of Duet HUM-130 ; 2 is Bandleader HUM-129; 3 is Street Singer HUM-131. No. 4 resembles Little Fiddler HUM-2 & 4, only without the umbrella and with a top hat substituted for the derby. No. 5 is Serenade HUM-85, and No.6 is Soloist HUM-135. It is possible that there are others in this series.

Children

Children figurines comprised the bulk of ceramics exported for the dime store trade. Many, however, were of a good quality while others were just what one would have expected to find there.

Top row: A 5" H. accordian player; a 4¾" H. girl in a costume reminescent of Wales?; another accordian player, 4¼" H. **Middle row**: A man with bow tie and top hat holding an ice cream cone, 4⅝" H.; a child wearing a white coat with his hands in his pockets, 3¾" H. **Bottom row**: A reclining Asian, possibly Korean, 3" H., 3½" W.; a tiny girl sits playing with her sand pail, 2" H., nicely glazed; a girl shelfsitter reading a book, the seated portion is 2" H.

Children musicians. **Top row**: *Highly glazed tuba and accordian players, 5¼″ H.; a three-piece band, 4″ to 4½″ H.* **Middle row**: *Nos. 1 and 3 are 4⅝″ H. flute players from same mold; a 4½″ H. boy plays his mandolin; a 3¾″ H. drummer and a 4″ H. girl with a concertina.* **Bottom row**: *Nos. 1 and 2 are 2¾″ H.; the boy with violin is 4″ H.; the last two are similar, but there is a difference. They are 3¼″ H.*

Top row: *A girl holding bowl with milk spilling from it is 5¼" H. A boy boxing with fists in front of face is 4¾" H. A 4" H. girl holds a skirt filled with flowers.* **Middle row**: *Pair of Dutch children. 4¼" H.* **Bottom row**: *Girl with doll and carriage, 2¾" H. The girl with basket sitting on fence with dog underneath and the girl with book are 3" H.*

The six little girls, while small in stature, are big in appeal and have been dubbed "the girls in the polka dot dresses" by collectors.

The tiny boys have expressive faces as they play soccer. In another, a girl comes to her little brother's rescue. He looks a little worried. Probably more about her hitting him than getting stung by that bee.

A pair of 2¾" H. boys playing with balls. Frank Travis collection.

A little girl swatting a bee which is reposing on her brother's derriere. She looks determined while he looks worried. She is 4½" H. and is unglazed except for her orange jumper. He is 2¼" H. and is unglazed except for his white shirt. Blue MIOJ. It is difficult to find this pair together. She is also marked "10 cents" on the bottom.

*Each of these cute 3½" H. little girls with their big eyes are accompanied by an animal. **Top row**: Nos. 1 and 3 with duck are from the same mold with different decoration; No. 2, girl with bunny holds her skirt. **Bottom row**: Oriental girl with pig; girl with Keupie doll and kitten; Dutch girl with basket of flowers and puppy. All except #3 in top row have Mark #115.*

Representations of black people have become a hot collectible and some can be found in OJ. Many, however, such as the outhouse, are derogatory in nature while others, like the little boy, even though poorly painted, are cute.

A group of black figurines. These are highly sought after especially since a new group of collectors has emerged for any black memorabilia, not just OJ. **Top row**: *A rather tasteless bisque figurine showing a boy opening the door of an outhouse to find it already occupied. Printed on the front is NEXT; 2½″ H. A 4½″ H. girl holds an ear of corn as she stands alongside a corn planter.* **Bottom row**: *A 5″ H. farm boy and girl. He carries a rooster under his arm and she, a basket of vegetables; a 5¾″ H. shoe shine boy holds a brush in his hand, box reads SHINE 5 cents.*

A 4¼″ H. black boy with his hands behind his back. He is dressed the same as the pair of shelfsitters on page 75. Frank Travis collection.

The shelf-sitters are mainly figures of children. There are quite a few fishermen in this group. Perhaps they were made to perch on the edges of fish bowls. Many have lost their fishing poles. Shelf-sitters encompass all nationalities and every manner of play. Some have dolls, books and tennis rackets. These figurines are hard to find in pairs. Because of their precarious perches they were more prone to breakage than the regular statues.

An assortment of the ever popular shelfsitters. They include some Orientals, a cowboy and cowgirl, some children and some fishermen as well as a member of an angel band. Frank Travis collection.

Shelfsitters. **Top row**: A large Dutch girl shelfsitter, 6″ H. and a smaller Dutch boy, 5¼″ H. A 3″ H. black boy incised MIOJ on the seat of his pants. He sits on a wooden block stamped MIOJ. A 3½″ H. black boy and girl. **Middle row**: A Dutch boy with ships painted on his pants, gold shoes, 3½″ H. A boy with a brush and paint pot and girl with a doll, 5″ H. and a bluish-green MIOJ. A 3⅝″ H. Oriental man smoking a pipe. **Bottom row**: A 4¼″ H. bisque boy with MIOJ incised on back of shirt. A 4½″ H. bisque teenage boy. Both have lost their poles. A 4¼″ H. boy and girl with exceptionally long eyelashes. A 4¾″ H. Oriental boy with Mark #98. Yet another Oriental boy, 4½″ H. All shelfsitter measurements are from head to toe.

American Children

One of the most sought-after set of Occupied Japan collectibles is known as American Children. These statuettes, for the most part, are fine copies of the German Berta Hummel figurines.

They are usually marked "Occupied Japan" or "Made in Occupied Japan" in block letters with their titles and the words "American Children" inscribed on the bottom in cursive writing. At one time it was believed that all the figures should have the script printed in red and the block letters in black, but subsequent discoveries show that the color of the mark is not a prime factor in determining authenticity.

Over the past few years, American Children have become very popular with OJ collectors and bring high prices among collectors themselves, although there are many instances where these wonderful children have been found at flea markets and in antique shops for much less than an ardent collector would be willing to pay. American Children figurines are also found marked MIJ, but although they are twins to the MIOJ figures, are not considered collectible by OJ collectors.

The mark most commonly found on the bottom of the American Children figurines. Unless the piece is marked American Children, collectors do not consider it as such even if the figurine is identical to one which is marked.

*Top row: American Children, **Singing Teacher Boy, Singing Teacher Girl,** (No Hummel counterparts) 5⅝" H. **Bottom row:** American Children, **Just a Cactus** (Confidentally HUM-314) in red, OJ in black, 5⅝" H.; American Children, **Washing** (Wash Day HUM-321) MIJ in black, 5" H.; American Children **The Artist** (The Artist HUM-304) MIJ in black, 5½" H. I have given the Hummel counterparts in parenthesis and included two figurines which are marked MIJ. The Occupied Japan ones are identical to these.*

Many of these figures are exact copies of the Hummel figurines right down to their three eyelashes and they bear titles that closely resemble their German counterparts. Others take more liberty, but while not exact copies, compare with the Hummels and show that they were inspired by the original. These figurines are of as fine quality as the Hummels.

All of these American Children have their names and American Children written in red script and a black OJ. **Top row**: **Good Night** *(Doll Mother HUM-67),* 4⅞″ H.; **Little Astrologer** *(Stargazer HUM-132),* 4½″ H.; **The Doctor** *(Doctor HUM-127),* 5½″ H.; **Wanderer** *(Happy Traveler HUM-109),* 5½″ H.; **I Bring Greetings** *(Meditation HUM-13),* 5¾″H.; **The Kitty** *(Hummel counterpart unknown)* 5¼″ H.

Top row: American Children, The Leader *(Band Leader HUM-129) all in black, 5½″ H.; American* Children, Little Knight *(Prayer Before Battle HUM-20) in red, OJ in black, 4¾″ H.; American* Children, Little Cook *(Baker HUM-128) in red, OJ in black, 55/16″ H.* **Bottom row**: *American* Children, Shoemaker *(Boots-HUM 143) OJ all in red, 55/16″ H.;* American Children, News, *printed upside down, (Latest News HUM-184), OJ, all in black. 5⅜″ H.;* American Children, Goose Girl *(Goose Girl HUM-47) in red, OJ in black, 5⅜″ H. Margaret Bolbat collection.*

A checklist of 42 figurines has been compiled by the OJ Club, but as soon as it seems to be complete, another one of those pesky kids surfaces!

To date the list consists of:

Apple Thief, Bell Boy, Best Pals, Children Under Umbrella, Chimney Sweeper, Cradle Boy, The Doctor, Doll Mother, Going Home, Golfer & Dog, Goodnight, Goose Girl, Happy Traveler, I Bring You Greeting, In Concert, Just a Cactus, The Kitty, The Leader, Little Astrologer, Star Gazer, Little Cook, Little Drummer Boy, Little Knight, Little Shopper, Mailman, Meditation, News, Night Watchman, Painter, Photographer, School Girl, School Boy, Serenade, Shoemaker, Singing Birdies, Singing Teacher Boy, Singing Teacher Girl, Sweethearts, Tooth Ache, Wanderer, Washing, The Worshipper.

Stargazer and Little Astrologer are the same figurine. To further confuse us, this figurine has been found marked Little Astrologer with two figures on the same base. In addition to the boy peering through his telescope, a girl standing behind him points towards the sky.

While most of the figurines are in the same size range as the Hummels, 4¼″ to 6″, Sweethearts has been found measuring 7¼ inches tall. The majority of the American Children figurines have the same square or round cream-colored bases, but Little Drummer Boy, has been discovered on a brown latticed base.

Hummel-like Children

The Japanese potteries were most prolific when it came to copying Berta Hummel's lovely children. In many cases they did an admirable job. Collectors can create a superb collection, and a sizeable one too, if they limit themselves to these cute figurines. Matched up with the American Children and Hokutosha figures, they could fill several china closets and display cases to overflowing.

In some instances the boys and girls were duplicates of the Hummels. Others, while not exact copies, impersonate the originals which inspired them. Some of the more striking pieces of OJ fall into this category.

This delightful candy box is a copy of the MEL-6, CHILD IN BED. Figurines bearing the prefix MEL were Hummel prototypes bearing the last three letters of Hummel to identify them as such. This version is marked MIOJ but one has come to light marked American Children -Cradle Boy. This Mel figurine was never assigned a Hummel number. 4" H. x 5" W. Mark #40. Art Gill collection.

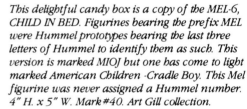

Top row: *This boy and girl with a sailboat doesn't have a Hummel counterpart but its Hummel-like figures could fool us into thinking that it is one. It is 5½" H. on a 3½" W. base with a blue-green MIOJ. Another view of the copy of Goose Girl HUM-47 pictured on page 81.*
Bottom row: *Two versions of Volunteers HUM-50. The larger stands 6" H. on a 2⅞" W. square base. The smaller is 5⅝" H. on a 3¾" W. oval base. Both have the brown lattice work on their bases. In the first the dog is located on the front. On the other he is alongside the drummer. Blue-green MIOJ marks. All these figurines have the three eyelashes indicative of the genuine Hummels. The smaller courtesy of Jessie Lange.*

The first figurine is a copy of *Angelic Sleep* (HUM-25). The Hummel figurine includes a candleholder which is omitted in this copy. The angel is 3⅛" H. on a 4" W. base and has a bluish-green mark. The second figurine of a woodland girl, with no Hummel counterpart, is another exceptional piece of craftsmanship. The piece is highly glazed and the features are well defined. She is playing a metal flute and there are two bunnies behind the mother rabbit. She is 4" H. on a 3½" W. base.

Top row: The boys are 6" H. Although their Hummel counterparts are unknown, they are very German in appearance. The figure of three girls on a single base is a loose copy of *Schoolgirls*, HUM-177. Although some of the details are missing, there are also similiarities. 6¼" H. including the 5¼" W. base. **Bottom row**: No. 1 is a faithful copy of *Joyful* HUM-53, 3¾" H.; No. 2 resembles *Meditation* HUM-13, but is minus the basket, girl stands 5" H. and has Mark #26; No. 3 girl stands 5½" H. and carries a knapsack and umbrella.

The Goose Girl is probably one of the most copied of the Hummel figurines...not only in OJ, but by many others too.

Although some figures do not have exact Hummel counterparts, it is apparent from their configurations that they were inspired by similar members of the Hummel family.

The pair on the top shelf have unusual large feet which look like they are clad in oversized slippers; No. 1 on the bottom shelf is the copy of Goose Girl HUM-47. This was a very popular Hummel figurine and was widely imitated by others. 5¼" H. on a 3¼" W. base. Mark #89; the second figurine shows a girl in a Tyrolean costume taking her dog for a walk, or is it the other way around? She stands 5" H.

Top row: *All are 4¼″ H. and are variations of Hummel figurines.*
Middle row: *No. 1 is 4⅜″ H. Nos. 2 and 3 are two different sizes of a Hummel-like hiker. One is 4⅝″ H. and the other is 4¼″ H.*
Bottom row: *No. 1 is 3⅜″ H., No. 2 is 3¾″ H. and 3 is 4″ H. The*

Dutch girl is one half of a set of porcelain bookends. Her companion is a Dutch boy. She is 3¾″ H. The first figurines in the middle and bottom rows are marked with a bluish-green MIOJ on bottoms that are partially unglazed.

Top row: *5½″ H. Newsboy. Pile of papers on ground are painted NEWS with lines to resemble newspapers. Girl with puppy and kitten holds a bottle and a cup. She stands 5¾″ H. on a 2¾″ W. base. This girl has the most wonderful eyelashes. A very naughty 5¼″ H. girl hits a boy over the head with her umbrella. The 4″ H. boy plays the ukulele and has a bluish-green MIOJ mark.* ***Middle***

row: *A 4″ H. girl lifts her little sister to drink from the bubbler. The boy with a puppy and the girl with a duck are a 3¾″ H. pair; The ice skater with hands on hips stands 3½″ H. and is marked twice with red MIOJ.* ***Bottom row***: *Three skiers. Nos. 1 and 3 have mark #98. The first is 4½″ H.; the others are 4″ H. No. 1 is loosely copied from Skier HUM-59.*

*An assortment of Hummel look-a-like children. They range in size
from 2¾" to 6" H.*

Ceramic Sets

One of the more challenging aspects of collecting OJ is attempting to complete some of the porcelain and bisque sets that were made. A stumbling block is that sometimes we do not know what or how many constitutes a set. Everytime it seems that a set is complete another piece surfaces.

The bisque sets of boys would be fabulous accessions for any collection. One is a set of angels while the other set features putti (wingless cherubs).

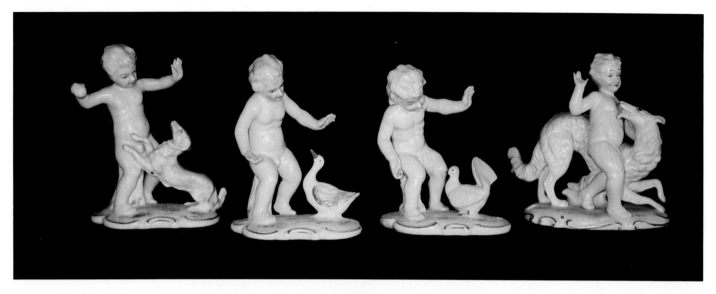

Four bisque curly-haired boys playing with animals. Two have dogs, one has a duck and the other a chicken. 5" H. on 6" W. bases. Mark #71. Wayne Walters collection.

Four bisque angels with wings pose in various positions with their donkeys. 3½" to 5" H. Mark #9 in gold. Wayne Walters collection.

Frog collectors will admire these sets of frogs; especially the humanoid ones. Many multi-figured sets were produced.

Top row: A pair of bug-eyed frog planters, 3½" H. The first has the opening in the back, while the second hugs an opened flower. *Bottom row*: A set of four humanoid frogs in a variety of posture, seated frogs are 2¼" H. and the others 2" to 2½" H. All have Mark #106.

Top row: Parts of three different porcelain clown sets. The only difference in Nos. 1 and 2 are their heights. The smaller one is 4¾" H.; all the others are 5" H. *Bottom row*: A 6½" H. court jester with ruddy cheeks raises his hand in greeting. A polka-dotted clown astride a pig is of exceptionally fine quality. 5" H. and 4⅜" W. This clown also comes accompanied by a begging dog. Mark #9. The reclining clown rests his chin on his hands. 2¾" H. x 4½" W. This clown comes in several other poses. Mark #95.

Top row: *Three 4⅛" H. turbanned Indian boys. The one with the red turban carries a jug and a basket of fish; the blue turbanned boy carries vegetables and fruit and a basket containing two bottles while the white turbanned boy is accompanied by a pig. The next two figures are copies of the famous Meissen monkey band. They are 3¾" H. and 3⅞" H. This set also comes in a slightly larger size.* **Middle row**: *A four member duck band, 3" H. Each wears a different color hat. Small 1¾" H. white monkeys with green jackets comprise another monkey band.* **Bottom row**: *The two Eskimos with dogs and blue parkas are 3⅛" H. The seated Eskimo in the center with the fishing pole and fish wears a green parka. Three more monkey musicians, 2½" H. Each is topped by a different colored hat.*

Top row: Three 3" H. angel shelf sitters. **Middle row**: All these
figures plus No. 3 in the bottom row make up an angel band. They
comprise a set since all their bases are identical. They are 3⅛" H.
Bottom row: A seated concertina playing angel is 2½" H.; the
3¾" H. middle figure is not a musician but rather a putti without
wings holding a sheaf of wheat.

The porcelain girls are found in many poses and, when their dresses are painted in different colors, many of these same poses can be counted as an addition to the set. The little naked girls with their topknots are equally as charming and fun to look for.

Top row: *The same ruddy-cheeked girl with bud vases in various poses is of a very highly glazed porcelain. Nos. 1 and 4 are from the same mold but have different colored dresses and flowers. They are 2⅞" H. on 4" W. bases. The square and round pieces are 3⅝" H. All are marked with a red MIOJ and an incised EL inside a flower.* **Middle row**: *Nos. 1, 3 and 5 are marked as above. No. 1 is reading a book and No. 5 holds flowers. No. 2 naked girl has a red MIOJ and No. 4 has Mark #59. They are both 3" H. and standing on books.* **Bottom row**: *More naked girls. The two bud vases are 2½" H. on 3⅛" W. bases. The reclining girls have their elbows resting on books. Mark #59. The center figure is part of the set pictured below.*

Four porcelain naked girls play musical instruments. They are 3⅝" H. The girl on the left is the only one who has wings and has her hands over her ears! They all wear flowered headpieces. The identical bases tell us they are a set. Frank Travis collection.

Another interesting set are these bees or bugs. Since they come in several sizes, a large number of figures make up this set. They adorn vases and planters as well as salt and pepper and condiment sets.

These little fellows are referred to as bees, bugs, ladybugs and insects. Personally, I feel that the ones who have spotted wings are ladybugs and the rest are bees. You decide. **Top row**: A four-piece condiment set consists of two Indians and a tepee in a canoe. The Indian chief is 2¼" H. and the squaw is 2" H., both marked Japan; the tepee is unmarked and 2½" H. with a removable top; the canoe is 6¾" W. and marked MIOJ. The planter with the bug alongside is 4" H. x 6" W. Mark #50. **Middle row**: A bee playing a guitar; a newsboy; a lady with a kerchief wrapped around her head; a hobo with a black leaf hat, with a decal that proclaims him a souvenir of Cypress Gardens, Florida; and a bee playing a horn are all 4" H. **Bottom row**: These smaller figures range in height from 2¼" to 2¾". They include a sad boy with a cap; a bug eating; a baseball player; a newsboy; a cigar-smoking bug wearing a derby; an Indian chief with a peace pipe; and a bug with a leaf bat playing the violin.

The elves are found in many postures and are incorporated in several different items. They generally have ruffled collars, some of which have not withstood time or worn very well.

The Japanese prove their aptitude for imitating the goods of others in little figures resembling German woodcarvings. The complete set of 12 Dickens characters was fashioned after the Royal Doulton originals.

Five 3⅝" H. men were molded to appear to be German wood carvings. Nos. 1 and 5 are similiar but colored differently.

*These elves with their leaf hats are very engaging. **Top row:** Planter is a flower blossom. 4" H. with Mark #106. The striding elf waves and is composed of a nice quality porcelain. He has the three eyelashes found on the Hummels, 4½" H. **Bottom row:** All three of these seated elves are 3" H. and have Mark #106. Their ruffles are edged in gold. Where the ruffles meet in the front, they appear to be damaged but since this is evident on all the elves I have come across, I believe that they should be this way.*

Opposite page

*A complete set of 12 Dickens characters fashioned after the Royal Doulton originals. The Japanese, however, made some errors in translating some of the titles. **Top row:** Little Dorrit, Mr. Pickwick, Betsy Prigg, Mr. Micawber. **Middle row:** Captain Cuttle, Dolly Varden, Artful Dodger, Sydney Carton. **Bottom row:** Fat Boy, Bill Sakes, Mrs. Camp, Tonny Wellen. They are all 4⅜" H. with their names inscribed in gold cursive writing across the front of the bases.*

Decorative Plates

The Japanese talent for fine painting is reflected in the many handpainted decorative plates which they exported to this country. Some are artist signed. Many are made from molds which incorporate holes on the back to run ribbon or twine for hanging them on the wall while others have reticulated edges through which ribbon could be threaded.

This handpainted plate with swans in the foreground has Mark #85 and is also signed by the artist, T Kato. 9⅛" W. Margaret Bolbat collection.

This plate is decorated with another scene painted and signed by the artist T Kato. It is 9⅛" W. and is marked Ucagco China MIOJ. Margaret Bolbat collection.

An unusual 8⅜" square plate with reticulated corners. The scene is similar to those above and signed by the same artist. Mark #98. Margaret Bolbat collection.

Ones marked Chuba China are thick with gold decoration and with vibrantly colored flora. Flowers and trees were a favorite subject for handpainted plates.

This 7¾" plate is an example of a white porcelain blank used for china painting. The artist has painted an amateurish floral decoration on it. Mark #27. Margaret Bolbat collection.

Three plates with reticulated edges. The larger is 8⅜" in diameter and the smaller two measure 6¼". Mark #16. Margaret Bolbat collection.

Two Satsuma-like plates featuring oriental tree designs, 7⅝" in diameter. Marked all in gold with MIOJ and an oriental symbol. Margaret Bolbat collection.

Two square porcelain plates with peonies and orchids. Gold edging, 7½" in diameter. Mark #23. Margaret Bolbat collection.

Plates are also found with pastoral scenes and landscapes...some of which have oriental overtones. Not all plates are round, but come in other geometric forms.

This 10" handpainted plate is a typical Japanese scene with Mt. Fujiyama in the background. Marked HP Shofu China (decal) in black and purple, MIOJ in black. Margaret Bolbat collection.

Another 10" handpainted plate with a tranquil forest scene. Mark #85. Margaret Bolbat collection.

Set of 4" H. coasters with 3⅜" H. stand. Each coaster is painted with a different scene. Each marked with H.P. over a capital D flanked by a branch of leaves over MIOJ. Margaret Bolbat collection.

A 7¼" W. octagonal shaped plate with typical oriental decoration. The dish is 8½" long, 6¾" W. and sits on a ¾" deep foot. Both have enameled designs and are marked with black Japanese-like characters enclosed in a green square with MIOJ in red. Margaret Bolbat collection.

The portrait plates are just one more example of the imitative ability exhibited by the Japanese potters. Copies of the Italian series, they defy detection as replicas until the backstamp is read.

*Row 1: These plates are copies of an Italian set. 6¼" W., all have Mark #81. The names of the subjects left to right are: Beatrice Cenci, Pauline Bonaparte and Baby Stuart. **Bottom row:** No. 1 has Mark #4 while No. 2 has Mark #81. No.1 is a self portrait of Raphael and the other is Beatrice D'Este.*

Companions to the larger plates above. These plates are 4" W. The first one has Mark #81 and all the others Mark #4. The middle plane in row one is a portrait of Fabriola.

Rare pieces exist which reflect Japanese motifs in their decoration. For example, the subtlety of the reeds through which the fish swim is indicative of oriental art as are the skillfully decorated butterfly bowls.

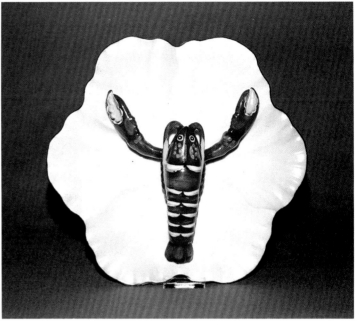

A large serving dish with a realistic lobster decoration measures 9¾" x 9". It is marked in gold with a capital G and two leafy branches. Margaret Bolbat collection.

The 5" deep bowl with fish design has a very Japanese appearance. The fish swim through delicate green reeds. It has a blue reticulated outer edge and is marked with a light blue MIOJ. Frank Travis collection.

A set of five 4½" wide shallow bowls with a different butterfly pictured on each. Marked Saji Handpainted OJ in blue. Josephine Stine collection.

Vases and Planters

Down through the ages man has required vessels to hold his flowers and plants. The Japanese never thought for a moment that Americans had moved away from that need. They inundated the market with vases and planters of dubious artistic value as well as some that were wonderful to behold.

Tiny vases were sold in the dime and variety stores to children who had only a dime to spend on a present for their mother's birthday. Quite often, these little vases were very attractive...other times they left a lot to be desired aesthetically.

A collection of small porcelain vases. **Top row**: *2½"H. slip-decorated dragon vase; the next three vases are 2⅝" H. and are decorated with landscape scenes; an orange slip-decorated dragon vase, 2⅝" H.* **Middle row**: *The first three were packaged as a set in a single box and are decorated with cats, bunnies and ducks. They stand 2¼" H.; this 3½" H. vase has crudely painted on the front "Irene & Jose"; a flowered 2½" H. vase.* **Bottom row**: *2½" footed vase marked H. Kato MIOJ; a 2½" footed vase with Mark #72; 2¾" H. handled vase with applied flower; a mirrored image pair of vases, 3" H., seated lady on front.*

A 9½" H. pair of Kutani-type mirror image vases painted in rust and gold on a white background. They have traditional Japanese decoration with branches, flowers and birds. The reverse side shows a bird in flight. They measure 4" across the opening and 15¼" at their widest part. Marked MIOJ under a picture of Mt. Fuji. Art Gill collection.

An 8½" H. powder blue vase covered with handpainted butterflies and flowers. It stands on a 3¼" base and has a 3" opening. Marked Banko China MIOJ with CPO in a diamond. The 5" H. vase with a gold dragon painted on it is marked with an illegible name then China, Occupied Japan and E-W in a circle. The base is 1⅞" round and the opening is 2". The ornate 6½" H. vase has a slip-trailed dragon attached to it, a 2⅜" round base and a 2" W. opening. It is trimmed with gold and white beading. These are three examples of the finer quality vases to come out of Japan during the occupation.

This 7⅝" H. pink and maroon vase has the excessive gold decoration so characteristic of those pieces bearing the Chuba China decal. Mark #16. It is formed from leaves standing upright on a 3" round gold base. Margaret Bolbat collection.

The brown vases are good examples of those poorly made ones while others would be welcome additions to anyone's collection. The Satsuma-like vases are some of the more commonly found of the period. Although similar in design, often the slightest variation makes them dissimilar...proof that they were truly handpainted.

An assortment of Satsuma-type vases. **Top row**: *These six vases range in size from 2" to 3¾". They are adorned with both Geisha girls and men. The second one is marked Kashihara.* **Middle row**: *All these vases are 2½" H. Nos. 2 and 5 are marked Kashihara.* **Bottom row**: *The first is decorated with a slip dragon, 2½" H.; a handled vase, 2½" H.; 2" H. vase, unusual in that the background is all one color; two 2½" H. vases with men figures. No. 4 is marked Kashihara.*

Top row: *Nice quality 4¾" H. vase, Mark #46 minus Meiko China; 6" H. vase with flower decal; a blue vase with gold handles, 5½" H.* **Bottom row**: *A 3¼" H. brown vase featuring a pink nude on the front; 2½" H. vase with an allover floral design; 3¾" H. vase with Mark #72; another brown vase, 3" H.*

Vases with decals or labels on them proclaimed they were souvenirs of a vacation at Niagara Falls, or Newport, R.I. They came in all shapes and sizes copying Wedgwood, Mexican pottery and Italian majolica. In addition, there were some highly original ones.

The figural vases may hold either real or dried flowers. There are many varieties of vases to be found and these can constitute the basis for an eclectic collection. Majolica and Capo-Di-Monte copies show good examples of some of the quality vases which can be found.

Top row: A 4¼" H. nicely decorated bulbous vase marked "SGK flower basket Moriyama Allied Forces" in red, a twisted rope around the middle ends in a tassel on the back; 6½" vase resembling Mexican pottery, the design is incised into the surface; 4¼" H. vase with slip-decorated flowers, decal says "Souvenir of Newport, R.I.". **Middle row**: Three two-handled vases with a great deal of applied gold decoration ranging in size from 2¼" to 2¾", all marked with Mark #109. **Bottom row**: 2¾" H. Wedgwood-like vase with applied rose; 4" H. vase with parrot in relief on front; 3½" H. souvenir vase with a transfer decal from Niagara Falls.

Three figural vases. An English granny with a basket and umbrella has an opening in the back of her head. The second figure could be "Mary, Mary Quite Contrary". She wears a wide-brimmed gardening hat and carries flower clippers in her hand. The opening is a basket filled with dried straw flowers. The third is a wide-eyed girl wearing an apron. The bowl she holds is the receptacle for flowers. All three are 5" H.

8⅛" H. white porcelain vases with dark green decoration on the fronts depicting a lady with a cherub and a man holding his hat. The same lady with the cherub decorates the reverse side of the vases. Mark #45. Frank Travis collection.

The heavy embossing on these pieces enhances the decorating. The 8" H. vase has a similiar pattern to the 6" H. vase but the difference in colors makes them appear totally unalike. The Capo-Di-Monte style 8" H. lamp bases with the small hole in the top for the lamp rod are shaped and decorated in a classical Grecian style. Josephine Stine collection.

Planters have always been very popular with housewives. Many of the OJ planters are pleasing. There was, however, a propensity towards making donkey cart planters (with an occasional bunny or oxen) of every posture and size imaginable. These are very easy to find at flea markets and garage sales and quite often are passed over by the more sophisticated collector, yet there are those collectors who like to add them to their collections.

Some unusual cart planters. **Top row**: *A young, wide-eyed donkey pulls this gaily decorated cart, 6¾" W. with Mark #111; a 7½" W. planter with donkey and cart.* **Middle row**: *This cart is being pulled by a bunny! Probably held an Easter plant. It's 7½" W. with Mark #111; a nicely colored cart pulled by a pony, 7¼" W. with Mark #89 in black.* **Bottom row**: *This perky jackass pulls a round cart, 4" W.; an oxen-drawn 7½" W. cart has Mark #111; a small 4½" W. donkey and cart.*

Besides the retail market, there was a demand for planters from florists. The once-popular dish gardens could have been planted in the oblong planters. Christmas ones have been found, and for new mothers ones shaped as pink and blue baby booties. Figural planters were very popular. Children and animals comprise the bulk of their decoration. Planters are found in both porcelain and bisque, with the bisque ones showing the better craftsmanship.

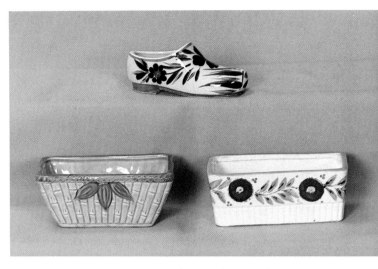

*Animal planters. **Top row**: A pair of 4½" H. dogs flank a 4" H. sad-eyed dog, Mark #112. **Middle row**: A cat with a blue bow has Mark #112, 5½" H.; a walking dog with a basket weave planter is 3" H. **Bottom row**: Slipper with kitten is 3" H. x 4¾" W.; a bunny pulling a cart, Mark #112, 3" H. x 5¼" W.*

*__Top row__: A slipper planter gaily decorated to resemble Mexican pottery, 2½" H. x 5½" W. **Bottom row**: Two rectangular planters for dish gardens. Both have Mark #112. The openings measure 3½" x 6".*

Figural planters. **Top row**: *Seated coolie, 2½" H. x 3½" W.; lady holding skirt, flat features, 4⅝" H. x 3¾" W.; sleeping Mexican peasant clasping guitar, 2" H. x 3" W.* **Middle row**: *Seated boy with dog, 3½" H. x 2¾" W.; seated boy and girl on bench, Mark #72, 3¼" H. x 2½" W.; dancing lady, open in back for flowers, 4½" H.* **Bottom row**: *Hummel-like girl in prayer at roadside shrine,greenish MIOJ, 5" H. x 4¼" W.; lady holding fan with flower-shaped cart, 4½" H.*

Opposite page bottom:

This dinner set consists of cups and saucers, dinnerplates, luncheon plates, soup dishes and sauce dishes. In addition there are several serving pieces. It is very colorful with its blue border and centered bouquet of flowers. Marked Made by Richi China.

Eat, Drink and be Merry

This chapter encompasses all those dinner sets, tea sets, demitasse sets, cups and saucers and any other dishes with which the Japanese flooded the market. They made an incredible amount of dinner ware. It is amazing how many different patterns there are.

A small display of the many blue and white dishes found marked MIOJ. **Top row:** *A 9¼" W. dinner plate with MIOJ and a crown; a 9½" W. grille plate, Mark #62; a 9⅛" W. dinner plate marked MIOJ in blue.* **Middle row:** *A full size cup and saucer with the dragon pattern made of fine china with a blue MIOJ; a 7¼" W. dessert plate, marked in blue N.K.T. MIOJ; a cup and saucer (part of a dinnerware set) Mark #34.* **Bottom row:** *A 5¾" W. saucer, marked Maruta China MIOJ featuring a European scene of a man with a cart and a cathedral in the background; a full sized Willow Ware cup and saucer with a blue MIOJ; a small cup and saucer, featuring the Phoenix Bird pattern, with a blue MIOJ. The cup measures 2¾" in diameter, the saucer 4⅜".*

Many of the dishes are not marked with the names of the patterns causing collectors to invent their own, but there are quite a few that are marked. Some marks on these dishes include Aladdin "Minuet"; Bienville Regal China; Cherry China; Crown Ivory China; Empire Shaped Meito China; Fuji China "Rosette"; and Gold Castle.

Grace "Rochelle"; Harmony House (Sears & Roebuck's trademark) Meito China "Prince Edward"; Holly China "Laurel"; Hudson; "Iris"; Meito China "Chatham"; Meti China "Ivory China"; Mikado China "Dresden"; Mikado China "Malay"; Mikado China "Laurel"; and Mikado China "Patio".

Also Monarch China; Narumi "Princess Pattern" made by Sango; Noritake; Norleans China "Chatham"; Orian Fine China; Meito Norlean's China "Rosanna"; Richi China; Rose China (made by Noritake); Sango "Silver Poppy"; Ucagco China "Apple Chintz"; Victoria "New Dawn"; and Yoto China "Gold Crest." These are only some of the many backstamps we can find on OJ dinnerware.

The Japanese Trade Guide of 1949 tells us that of all the chinaware and porcelain exported between September 1947 and April 1948, tableware accounted for over 90%.

SCAP Schedule "A," dated August 15, 1947, of merchandise and products available from stock for exportation lists dinner sets of ninety-three, sixty-three and fifty-three pieces, also tea sets, coffee sets and plates and saucers. (Where are the cups?).

This luncheon set of fine china consists of eight full-sized cups and saucers, eight 7½" cake plates, a 7" H. teapot, 4½" H. sugar and 4" H. creamer. Mark #83 minus the handpainted script.

This demitasse set for six is fashioned in the Capo-Di-Monte style. The lids of the coffee pot and sugar have fish finials. The inside of the cups are gilded with a flower design. The coffee pot is 8" H., the sugar is 4" H., the creamer is 3½" H., the cups are 2¼" H. and the saucers measure 4¾" in diameter. They bear the SGK decal with Handpainted OJ written in script.

Sets were made up of place settings for six, eight or twelve. The more place settings, the more serving pieces included. Settings for twelve made up the ninety-three-piece sets, eight-place settings gave you sixty-three pieces, while the six-place settings have fifty-three pieces. A place setting includes a dinner plate, a cup and saucer, dessert and bread and butter plates, and soup bowls. Sometimes a sauce dish was substituted for the dessert plate. Serving pieces consisted of sugars, creamers, gravy boats, platters and vegetable dishes, both covered and uncovered.

Brown pottery teapots were manufactured for both home use and restaurant use. The individual, one-cup pot was one that was used in many of the restaurants of the day. The Hokutosha pottery also made some dinner ware after the Imari pattern.

Five brown pottery teapots with varying capacities. **Top row:** *Three-cup and six-cup pots are decorated with enameled flowers. They are both marked with M over G in yellow.* **Bottom row:** *One-cup restaurant quality pot and one-cup pot with painted embossed flower, both marked with embossed Occupied Japan; two-cup pot with enameled flowers and T over M mark in yellow.*

This sugar and creamer have Mark #50 and are copies of the Japanese Imari china. The creamer is 3½" H. and the sugar is 4" H. The 8" plate has Mark #32. Margaret Bolbat collection.

Cup and saucer collecting has become a specialized aspect of OJ collecting. There are many collectors who hunt only for these. They come in demitasse size, in full size, and even in over-sized novelty cups.

Top row*: A set of four demitasse cups are of the same pattern but each is decorated with a different color. The 1½" H. cups have four panels, two picture a lady and gentleman, and the others a floral pattern. The 3¼" square saucers have four panels of flowers plus a flower in the center. They bear Mark #32.* ***Middle row****: A dainty cup with a fluted 3¾" round saucer is 1½" H.; a 2¼" H. cup and 4½" round saucer in an all-over blue floral pattern; a typical Japanese lustreware cup and saucer with a landscape scene, 3½" saucer and 1¾" H. cup; a 2" H. cup with alternating gold and flowered panels and a 4½" round saucer.* ***Bottom row****: A 2¼" H. cup with a 4¼" saucer with floral pattern; a six-sided cup and saucer, three panels of gold on maroon and three with flowers. Cup is 2½" H. and saucer measures 4½" in diameter; 1¾" H. cup with a 4⅞" saucer covered with a pretty bird pattern; a 2" H. cup with 3¾" saucer is enhanced by its gilt decoration. Mark #21.*

These full sized coffee/tea cups with 5½" diameter saucers are just a very few of the hundreds that appear to have been manufactured. One could amass a sizeable collection of just cups and saucers marked MIOJ. **Top row**: Left to right: Strawberries and flowers decorate this cup and saucer. The footed cup has a large orange and white flower on a blue-green background with gold decoration. Both have Mark #91. The third sports a large yellow flower and has Mark #55. **Second row**: Cup and saucer banded with pink and blue peonies has Mark #57. A super abundance of gold decorates the second set with its alternate bands of maroon and gold trim. Mark #78. A Grecian type band of red, white and blue enhances the last set. If you drink all your tea you will discover a flower in the bottom of the cup. It has Mark #34. **Third row**: No. 1 is a slip-dragon decorated cup and saucer with M in a wreath mark. No. 2 is a dainty teacup with a garden gate decoration. No. 3 has a floral rim and Mark #91. **Bottom row**: The exterior of this cup is black and gold with a floral design on the saucer and the inside of the cup. Marked with a gold Phoenix bird over an E. The second cup has a pink saucer and exterior with a floral design inside the cup. Mark #14 in gold. Betty and Mike De Arruda collection.

Two oversized novelty cups. "Double or Nothing" cup is marked Halsey MIOJ. The "Father" cup sold for $5.75 a dozen wholesale. There is also a "Mother" cup. Both cups are 4" H. on 7¾" saucers. Art Gill collection.

There is also a wide range of blue and white cups and saucers, besides the Willow and Phoenix Bird, that have come to light.

The coffee service with its French inscription was more than likely manufactured for the French-Canadian market.

Three blue and white cups and saucers. Nos. 1 and 2 have the Maruta China mark. The peacock design set has a 5½" saucer. The center set, Hawthorne design, a 5" saucer and is marked MIOJ in blue. The Blue Willow set has a saucer measuring 5¼". Margaret Bolbat collection.

All three of these cups and saucers are regular-sized. The first two are marked Maruta and have 5½" diameter saucers while the third is 5⅛" W. and has a blue MIOJ. Margaret Bolbat collection.

Three espresso or demitasse cups and saucers. The first has gold trim and Mark #34. The others have blue MIOJ. Saucers are 4⅜", 3⅞" and 4⅝" W. Margaret Bolbat collection.

This ornate demitasse set consists of 15 pieces, a 7½" H. coffee pot, a 3¾" H. sugar bowl, a 2½" H. creamer and six 2" x 2¼" cups with 4½" round saucers. On both sides of the pot appear a poem written in French. "Noir comme le diable, chaud comme l'enfer, pur comme un ange, doux comme l'amour, recette le rareecrand." Translated into English it reads "Black like the Devil, Hot like Hell, Pure like an Angel, Sweet like Love, Recipe of Rareecrand." It is quite possible that this decoration was applied to this set with our French Canadian neighbors in mind. Mark #61. Frank Travis collection.

Miscellaneous dishes and plates were also exported during that time. It staggers the imagination to think of the multitude of dishes to search for!

The Japanese made enough dishes in the shape of leaves to cover an entire tree! They served as candy dishes, ashtrays, nut dishes, serving dishes, relish dishes, whatever the occasion called for. Here are just three. A double bowl leaf candy dish with a handle, 6½" L. and 6" W., marked SAJI, Occupied Japan, Fancy China with Handpainted written in green script; a 3½" W. nut dish with a red MIOJ, also gold O.H; possibly the artist's initials? The third is a 7½" L. oak leaf with acorns marked with Mark #94.

Mugs/Tobies/Animal Pitchers

OJ mugs come in many sizes and designs. Several varieties come with figural handles. There is one set whose handles consist of nude women. Another utilizes an Indian motif as decoration. Their handles are formed with the bent bodies of an Indian Chief and his squaw. There are also mugs which use a cowboy as the handle.

Two 5" H. mugs. A brave complete with headdress forms the handle of one while an Indian squaw provides a handle on the other. They are decorated with typical Indian scenes complete with tepees and canoes. Frank Travis collection.

Top row: *These two mugs both have figural handles. The first is a moonshiner and the second is a black South Seas native complete with spear. The first mug has a steer with horns on the front and is 5" H. Mark #107. the second is marked with a blue Handpainted surrounded by MIOJ. It measures 4⅜" H. to the top of the native's head.* **Middle row**: *A Capo-Di-Monte-type 3½" H. mug has winged cherubs cavorting in a vineyard. Mark #90. This Tom and Jerry mug is white with gold decoration. Has a blue MIOJ and is 2⅞" H.* **Bottom row**: *A plain barrel mug and the same mug embellished with grapes. Both are 4" H. Betty and Mike De Arruda collection.*

Others are Capo-Di-Monte and Tom and Jerry sets and the ordinary barrel mugs. The Japanese also made an attempt at producing German steins. Some are cruder than others. Others are authentic right down to their German legend.

The German characters on this 7⅝" high stein gives it an air of authenticity. One side shows a man seated on a tree stump with a standing woman. The handle is fashioned to form intertwined grape vines. Betty and Mike De Arruda collection.

The other side of the stein above shows an European house nestled in a pine forest. Betty and Mike De Arruda collection.

Top row: *A drinking scene in a tavern decorates this 6" H. beer stein. The second stein has a similar scene in dark brown against a dark green background. It is 5⅛" H. and has Mark #98 in black.* **Middle row**: *This 4½" H. mug has an Indian head motif. The second one has a handle simulated to look like wood, is 4¼" H. and features a bunch of grapes and their leaves.* **Bottom row**: *A 3½" H. pineapple mug with a bamboo-like handle. A mug with a hunting scene and a serpent handle stands 4" H. Betty and Mike De Arruda collection.*

Good workmanship is apparent in the Toby mug copies. They are very good copies of the real thing, such as the much sought-after MacArthur mug. Every collection should have a MacArthur mug, since he is so closely associated with the Occupation. Some Tobies are not only small in size but short on detail such as those with flatten features.

These copies of England's Royal Doulton Toby mugs are a good example of the ability of the Japanese to copy the wares of other countries. **Top row**: A 3" H. Dapper Dan with moustache; a 5" H. man winks at the barmaid; this 3¾" H. King Toby (sometimes called King David Toby) regally watches out over his kingdom. **Middle row**: A 3½" H. Toby with spectacles; a 1⅝" H. ashtray portraying a man with grannie glasses; the ever popular MacArthur mug stands 4¼" H. and is marked MERIT MIOJ in black. **Bottom row**: The 2¼" H. devil mug has a red Hand-painted MIOJ mark; the next three Tobies are 2⅝", 2⅜" and 2⅜" H.; a sad doggie is the subject of the 2⅛" H. mug.

For animal lovers, there is a nice set of animal-head pitchers. This is a nicely done series with very fine detail, even down to correct coloring.

A cow pitcher with the natural coloring associated with our conception of a brown bossy. The cream pours from her mouth, 4¼" H., Mark #94 in black.

Three porcelain animal creamers. The black and brown horses are both 4¾" H. The collie measures 4¼" H. All have Mark #87. Art Gill collection.

Miniatures and Novelties

The more easily found (and the most inexpensive) lie within this category. Here are the vast numbers of items made in the beginning of the Occupation for export to the US.

*Miniature porcelain novelty items. **Top row**: 2" lamp with Mark #72; 3¾" H. clock; 2" H. mantle clock. **Middle row**: 2¼" H. bowl of fruit; a 1¾" H. x 2½" W. piano suggests where the term piano legs might have originated; a 3" H. chair boldly decorated with flowers. **Bottom row**: A tiny 2¼" H. dresser; a 2¼" W. bed with a gold trimmed headboard and flowered spread; a 1¾" H. baby carriage decorated in relief with flowers.*

*Miniature vases, pitchers and novelties. **Top row**: A basket weave mini pitcher, 2⅞" H.; two clocks in the shape of teapots, similar faces but different times, 2" H.; 3¼" H. pitcher with decal reading "Lace Balconies, New Orleans". **Middle row**: A 2⅜" H. footed pitcher; Wedgwood-like 3½" H. pitcher; 2½" H. cornucopia; blue glazed teapot with applied flower, 1⅜" H. and a matching 2" H. coffee pot with no lid. **Bottom row**: Four mini decorated pieces, 2" H., trimmed in bright colors; a 2½" H. vase with a handle and spout; another teapot missing its lid, 1¾" H.*

An array of baskets and wheelbarrows. **Top row**: A 3¼" H. girl holding hat; boy pushing wheelbarrow, 2¾"H.; 3" Dutch girl holding a basket. **Middle row**: Five baskets ranging in height from 1¾" to 2½", all decorated with flowers. **Bottom row**: A 2" x 3½" wheelbarrow with floral decoration; 2½" H. basket decorated with grapes; 1½" H. wheelbarrow with applied flowers.

When the Japanese realized that these pieces were not selling as they had anticipated, they began to manufacture the better quality pieces. It seems a shame that they didn't realize this at the start...but then the collectible would be priced out of sight and new collectors wouldn't find anything to add to their collections. One of the benefits of collecting OJ is that if you specialize in these objects, you can amass a sizeable number without mortgaging the family homestead.

Once again, we have items that fall into another area of collecting; that of miniatures. Some of these pieces are an asset to a collection while others are rather crudely done.

Two porcelain miniature telephones show the evolution of the instrument. 2¼" H. These were some of the typical dime store knicknacks. Frank Travis collection.

Some objects are referred to as both toothpick holders and bud vases and can be used as either. This was part of the stock which was shipped to your local dime store.

Four pair of tiny bud vases or toothpicks. **Top row**: *A boy and a girl sit on barrels. 2½″ H.; a pair of Colonials play stringed instruments, 2⅝″ H.* **Bottom row**: *Two 2½″ H. clown toothpicks with Mark #72; a Dutch boy and girl push wheelbarrows, 3″ H. x 3⅜″ W.*

These little pieces have been labeled both toothpicks and bud vases. Regardless of what you call them, they are of interest to miniature collectors and those collectors who are short of display space. **Top row**: *An owl perched on a tree limb decorates this 2½″ H. piece; a 3⅛″ H. bud vase with a squirrel and a rooster; another squirrel on a tree trunk, 2⅝″ H.; a 2¼″ H. bluebird perched on a branch.* **Middle row**: *A 2¼″ H. Colonial man probably has a mate somewhere; a 2″ h. boy with a knapsack; a hunter with dog rides to the hunt, 2⅛″ H.; a 2⅝″ H. boy with a basket.* **Bottom row**: *A 2″ H. standing dog; a small swan dish with flowers measures 1½″ H.; a 2″ H. milkmaid with a cow.*

Some of the smalls, however, are of nice quality, including some interesting and unusual ones. This reinforces the premise that you must pick up everything and examine it...for you never know where you are going to see that mark!

An assortment of small porcelain figures. **Top row**: *Two pair of cherubs flank a mermaid reclining on a bed of shells. They measure 3¼″ H. The left cherubs hold grapes while the right pair are interested in the lovebirds at their feet. The mermaid is 3¾″ H. and 4″ W.* **Middle row**: *The miniature bisque pagoda, 1¾″ H. and the 3¼″ H. pagoda with palm trees were intended to decorate fish bowls. The 1⅜″ H. house has a mill wheel on the side.* **Bottom row**: *All four of these tiny pieces have elves on them. Nos. 1 and 4 are identical toy shops measuring 1⅜″ H. No. 2 has an elf sitting in a shoe house topped by a bluebird, 2″ H. No. 3 is a mushroom house with one elf peering out the window while two others stand at either side. 1¾″ H.*

*An interesting selection of celluloid miniatures. **Top row**: Donkey cart, 1½" H. x 2½" W.; dog and two puppies, ¾" H. x 1" W.; elephants on a wooden base,1" H. x 3½" W.; donkey cart, 1¼" H. x 2½" W. **Bottom row**: Seated dog, 1½" H. x 1" W.; elephant, 2½"H. x 3½" W.; windmill dog house pencil holder, stamped on bottom of house SONSCO, 2¾" H. x 2" W.; three dogs, 1" H. x 1¼" W. Art Gill collection.*

Ivory-like rickshaw with boy and passenger on a black base. 1½" H. x 1½" W. Frank Travis collection.

The three Art Deco ladies are among my favorites. They wear the wide-bottomed pants of the 20s and all three have floppy hats.

Three Art Deco ladies in a reclining position are dressed in circa-1920 wide bottomed pants and broad brimmed hats. The center vase is 3½" H. and the two figures measure 1¾" H.

Miniatures and novelties were made of other materials, too. The little plush animals have teeny tags around their legs. Folding paper fans were given away at parties as favors. The Union Jack favor has a mate in the Stars and Stripes. Other party favors and decorations were also made.

Top row: *Four plush chicks, 1½" to 1¾" H., have paper labels wrapped around one leg.* **Middle row**: *A plush chicken with a party hat, a baby chick and two roosters with feathers. A 2" x 3" Union Jack flag on a 5" metal staff has a paper label on the staff.* **Bottom row**: *A party favor honeycomb fan, 5" in diameter when opened, paper label on outside of wooden spine; 8" long bunch of cloth pink lilacs with label on stems.*

A group of party decorations and favors includes an expandable paper Japanese lantern, a mask, a miniature American flag, a yellow paper rose, a blue plush lei and the ever popular paper blowout. All are either stamped MIOJ or have paper tags. Art Gill collection.

A sampling of some of the Christmas items made for the American market. No. 1: A 4½" H. papier maché snowman with top hat has paper cutouts for his eyes and buttons. A red pipe cleaner circles his neck while white pipe cleaners act as arms. Purple MIOJ stamped on bottom. No. 2: A red plush wreath tree decoration with a foil candle, 3½" in diameter, has a paper label. No. 3: This 3⅛" H. St. Nicholas is dressed in a foil robe, trimmed with white pipe cleaners. He holds a candle, has a cotton batting beard and a paper label pasted on his back. No. 4 is a cluster of silvered glass beads, somewhat the worse for wear with several broken ones. Strung on wire, they have a paper label.

Christmas decorations (including glass ornaments and tree lights) flooded the market, but their fragility and the loss of their paper labels has narrowed the field. Time after time I pick up boxes of old Christmas balls at flea markets and church sales to find Made in the USA on them!

Kitchen Wares and Pottery

Many of these items were made in sets. One of the most popular is the Cottage set which consists of items that resemble Staffordshire cottage pieces. It includes a teapot, creamer and sugar, condiment set, cookie jar, cheese dish, and butter pats. A similar set is the Fireside set decorated with an old-fashioned fireplace. There are beehive sets fashioned after the Irish Belleek originals, oranges, windmills and many others. It can be fun (but also frustrating) to assemble one of these sets.

Porcelain salt and pepper shakes comprise a large group. It is not unusual for the shakers in three-part sets to be marked only "Japan," and the others to be unmarked. The trays marked MIOJ tell us that they are authentic. I wonder how many of these sets have become separated from their trays?

Opposite page:
An assortment of porcelain figural salt and peppers. **Top row**: *2¾" H. Indian chief and his squaw marked MIOJ; seated boy and girl, reading books, 2½" H.; seated East Indians, one playing the sitar, 3¼" H.* **Second row**: *Windmills, 2¼" H.; another American Indian pair, this chief has a much more detailed headdress, 2¾" H., marked OJ; a pair of violin playing pigs, 2⅜" H.* **Third row**: *3¾" H. dachshunds standing and begging; seated monkeys, 2⅜" H.; Hummel-like girl and boy. Boy holds a horse pull-toy and girl carries basket of flowers, 4⅛" H.* **Bottom row**: *2⅝" H. shakers decorated with Lilies of the Valley, this pair also comes in pink; Lady cook bell, 3⅛" H., marked inside; male cook egg timer, 3⅞" H.; girl and boy with animals and eye glasses, nicely done with expressive eyes, 3⅝" H.*

Top row: This cheese dish is part of a set referred to as the Cottage set. Other pieces to this set include a teapot, a covered sugar and creamer, condiment set on a tray (salt, pepper, and mustard) as well as a butter dish. The tray is 5½" x 7¼", Mark #88. The cover is 4¼" H., 5½" W. and 4" deep. **Bottom row**: *A beehive honey pot, 4" H. with a 3½" diameter bottom; a basket weave 2½" square jam pot on a 4¼" square bottom.*

Some of the covered dishes have basketweave bottoms. The hen on the basket is a familiar sight but the turkey is unusual. These pieces were painted with great care and in authentic colors.

Two fowl seated on baskets. The chicken measures 5" x 5" and the turkey is 6½" H., 7¾" W. and 5¼" deep. Both have Mark #50. Margaret Bolbat collection.

An assortment of salt and peppers. **Top row:** *A 3" H. red pepper; a 4¼" H. Oriental man carrying two 1¼" H. baskets, shakers are unmarked; a 3¼" H. Martha Washington shaker; 4¼" H. Aunt Jemina-type shaker, her missing partner wears a chef's outfit; a 3¾" H. windmill with rotating blades.* **Middle row:** *A 2½" basket holds a 1½" H. apple and lemon, shakers unmarked, basket has Mark #30; 2⅝" H. country man and woman bearing labels "Souvenir of Natchez, Miss."; doe and buck shakers, left one is 2½" W. and 2¼" H., marked Japan in black, the right one measures 2¼" W. x 2½" H., marked MIOJ in green; a country girl carrying a purse, 2⅝" H.* **Bottom row:** *3¾" H. Mexican pair; unmarked 2⅝" H. chicks in a nest, 3½"x 3" nest marked MIOJ; 3¼" H. turbanned East Indians seated, one with a zither.*

Multi-piece sets are very desirable and some are ingenious. For example, the lighthouse and the chef at the stove are good illustrations of this.

Some multi-piece salt and peppers and condiment sets. Height measurements are when sets are assembled. **Top row**: A chef stands at his 2½" W. stove. The pots are shakers, marked Japan. The top half of the chef removes to reveal the mustard pot with spoon. 5¼" H. with a blue R in circle, MIOJ. This Humpty Dumpty set is 3¼" H. and also comes in a larger version. The heads are unmarked shakers, Mark #9. Another condiment set has a lady's head as the cover to the mustard pot with an opening for its missing spoon. The flower shakers are marked Japan. 4⅛" H. with Mark #71. **Second row**: Gondola salt and pepper with all three pieces marked MIOJ. 2⅛" H. with a 5½" W. gondola. Two pigs in a poke are 2¼" H., pigs are marked Japan. The poke is 2⅝" H. A three-piece lighthouse set. The shakers are the lightkeeper's house and the second story of the lighthouse. Shakers are marked Japan and the set measures 3½" H. to the top of the lighthouse. **Third row**: An Indian serenades his squaw in a canoe. Indians are the shakers, marked Japan. The center of the canoe has a hollow for the mustard. Canoe is 6¼" W. and the set is 3" H. An elegant floral salt and pepper set. The flowers with gold butterflies on top are the shakers, marked Japan. They are 3¼" H. and the holder is 4" W., marked with a blue R in circle MIOJ. This porcelain set has unmarked shakers and measures 2⅛" H. to the top of the handle. The base of the holder is 2¼" W. **Fourth row**: A dainty four-piece condiment set with blue highlights and pink flowers. The shakers are the cream pitcher and the teapot. The mustard holder is the oversized sugar with lid. The tray is 6¼" W. and the mustard pot is 2¾" H. They both have Mark #107. An Irish Belleek copy, the beehive shakers with the bees atop are marked Japan. The holder is 4" W. and 3¼" H. to the top of the handle. Mark #88.

Chrome shakers and glass ones also exist. The metal ones are usually incised with the mark, and the glass ones are embossed on the bottom.

MIOJ pottery was among the few articles made for the American trade that can be said to be of Oriental design. Rice bowls exist in the familiar blue and white of Canton china, and some stoneware even has an Oriental symbol impressed on the bottom.

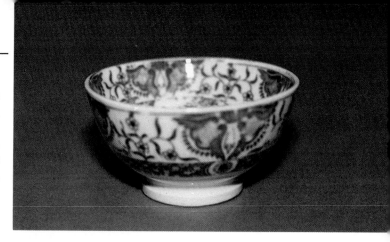

A blue and white rice bowl reminescent of Chinese Canton ware is 2½″ H. and 4½″ W. with a blue MIOJ. Art Gill collection.

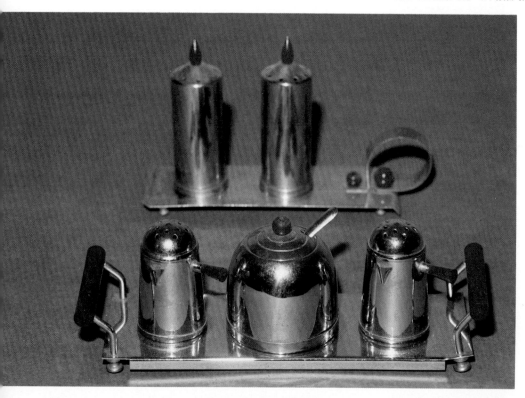

Two chrome salt and pepper sets highlighted with red plastic decoration. The Art Deco-like pair of candles are 3″ H. on a 5¼″ W. tray. The other set includes a condiment jar. It and the shakers are 2″ H. on a 6½″ W. tray .Frank Travis collection.

Three sets of pressed glass salt and pepper shakers. The first and last measure 2″ H. and have slightly different designs. The second pair with its red plastic tops are 2¾″ H. They all have MIOJ embossed on the bottom. Art Gill collection.

Some pieces are very Japanese in appearance. Pottery marked with the three mountains is of a superior quality. Several pieces have been found with orange and brown swirls and the texture is so smooth to the hand (much like Rookwood pottery) that it is difficult to stop stroking it.

A blue and white stoneware basket. The basket is 9" in diameter and 2½" deep. It is marked MIOJ in a circle, plus what looks like an impressed fan and a glazed oriental symbol. Margaret Bolbat collection.

Vividly colored bowl or vase. 4¾" H. and 6" in diameter. Marked MIOJ with three mountains underneath. Margaret Bolbat collection.

A mottled pottery vase. 4½" H. x 4¼" W. Stamped MIOJ in black. Margaret Bolbat collection.

Animals and Birds

Animal and bird figurines range from the poorly crafted to many finely crafted figures. As with many OJ items, they spill over into other collectibles. Many of us know persons who collect dog or cat figures...even elephants. With the staggering output of these OJ items, a collector who wishes to specialize in a certain animal or bird should have no trouble finding pieces to add to his collection; particularly if he chooses dogs.

A great variety of dog figurines exist. Unfortunately for cat lovers, there are not as many cats to be found, but there are some.

Top row: Reclining dog, 3½" W., 1¾" H.; seated dog, 3" W., 2½" H.; No. 3 standing dog, 4" W., 3½" H., Mark #88. **Middle row**: Barking dog, 5¼" W., 2¾" H.; standing terrier, 4" W., 3½" H.; both have Mark #88. **Bottom row**: Reclining dog, 5½" W., 3¼" H. This figure is of exceptional quality. Dachshund, 4½" W., 2¾" H.; both are marked MIOJ in blue.

Top row: Mother and puppy on a 5½" x 3¼" base, the adult dog is 6" H. and the puppy 4" H. **Middle row**: The dog eating from dish is 5¼" W. and 2¾" H.; the elongated dog measures 4½" from the tip of his nose to the tip of his tail. **Bottom row**: The little dog with a 2¼"H. basket is 2" W.; the sad-faced dog with the box of two puppies is 3¼" W. and 2⅛" H.; the dog with a shoe toothpick is 3" W.

Top row: First dog is 5" W. and 3¾" H., marked MIOJ in blue; No. 2 is 4" W. and 5" H., Mark #88. **Middle row**: No. 1 is 3½" W., 3¼" H.; No. 2, 2¾" W., 3½" H. with Mark #88. The pearlized dog is 4¼" W. and 3½" H. **Bottom row**: This cute 2½" W., 2¾" H. dog is looking at a gold fly on his tail. The planter is 2½" W., 3" H. and the seated dog is 2½" W., 2¼" H. with a blue MIOJ.

Top row: A regal Siamese cat sits upon a red cushion and guards his ball, 3½″ square with Mark #89 in black. **Middle row**: Three polka-dotted cats. 2″ H., 3″ long; 1½″ H., 2″ long; 2¼″ H., 3″ long. **Bottom row**: A cute 3¼″ H. Teddy Bear; a 2¼″ H. wide-eyed cat with a blue MIOJ.

Pig fanciers can find a few, as can elephant collectors. There were some tiny glass animals on the market, but because they had minute paper stickers, they are very difficult to find in today's market.

This little pig has a hole in the back that serves as a dispenser for cotton. 3¼″ H. Mark #33. Frank Travis collection.

*Two piggy banks with floral decoration.
2½″ H. Frank Travis collection.*

A herd of elephants; the double white elephants highlighted with gold stand 3¾″ H. with a red mark, their trunks have grooves in them but it is a mystery to me what their use is. The planter decorated with pink flowers is 3¼″ H. and has Mark #112. Two mini-elephants (one who lost his decoration, possibly washed away) are 1¾″ H. with a green MIOJ. The large pink planter also has Mark #112 and is 5″ H.; the brown ashtray set comes with three trays, each with a raised elephant in the center, the elephant is 2¾″ H. on a 6″ W. base, marked with a raised MIOJ; the 3¼″ round ashtray has Mark #89. They all have their trunks raised for good luck.

Top row: This seated pig with an opening on the back of his head stands 3⅜″ H. Mark #82. A piggy bank decorated to resemble Mexican or Italian pottery is 2¼″ H. and 3″ long. The black panda bear is 2¼″ H. **Middle row**: The first and last calves are similar but colored slightly different, 2¼″ long, they both have blue MIOJ's. The two glass figures are both 1¼″ H. and have paper labels. If you look closely you can see one on the tail of the blue rooster. The mini-dog in the center is 1½″ H. and 1″ W. and has MIOJ incised on his hip. **Bottom row**: The first deer has wonderful hand painted eyes that would just melt your heart, 4¼″ H. A Bambi-like reclining deer is 3″ x 3″ with a blue MIOJ. The lamb is either a small planter or vase, 3″ x 3″.

The forest animals with Mark #88 are good copies and seem to be more carefully made and more true to life.

We find the Japanese assigning human qualities to many of the animal figurines they manufactured. The frogs are unevenly painted bisque while the porcelain pigs and ducks (perhaps Daisy?) are of better quality.

A squirrel, bear cub and raccoon. These three forest creatures have very nice detail and coloring. They are 3" H. and have Mark #88. The pottery which employed this mark seems to have manufactured many nice animal figurines.

A pair of humanoid figurines, 4" long. The boy is watching the girl read a book. Frank Travis collection.

Two reclining bisque frog humanoid figures. 2" H. Frank Travis collection.

The bisque birds are some of the better quality bird figurines. Many are exquisitely made in both detail and color.

A popular subject was the waterfowl. Several of the planters are refugees from florist shops. Some large birds have definite oriental overtones. The storks and egrets were made in highly glazed porcelain. The tiny birds would be good pieces for those who have little space to display a collection.

Opposite page top:
Top row: *A 7⅛" H. Oriental bird colorfully decorated with flowers and a gold comb. A pair of storks, 3¼" H. and 2¾" H., Mark #109 minus the handpainted. A 3½" H. egret stands on one foot in marsh grass. A 2" H. butterfly on a 2¼" W. base with a wing span of 3¼".* **Bottom row**: *A flock of five birds ranging in height from 1⅜" to 2¼" and a 2½" H. owl.*

Opposite page bottom:
An array of bird and fowl planters. **Top row**: *A Bluejay and a frog eye each other across a log, Mark #116, 5" W. x 4¼" H.; a single Bluebird on a log, 3½" W. x 2¾" H.; a duck wearing an Easter bonnet, probably came from a florist shop, Mark #112, 6½" H.* **Bottom row**: *Chick with basket-weave planter, Mark #73, basket 2½" H.; newly hatched duckling wears part of his shell on his head, 4⅜" H., Mark #112; bird with gaily colored flowers adorns this 4½" W. x 4" H. planter.*

A collection of bisque fowl. The first pair of quail are 8" H. and 5" W. Mark #4. The three center birds (duck, owl, and kingfisher) are 5" H. and marked with Mark #94. The pair of peacocks are 9" H. and 4" W. and also have Mark #94. Wayne Walters collection.

A flock of nicely colored and glazed ducks and geese. **Top row**: *The planter is 4¼" W., 2" deep, and 3½" H., with a black MIOJ fired under a brown glaze.* **Bottom row**: *The three on the dark blue bases range from 2¼" H. to 3¼" H. The duck planter is 3½" H.*

During the 1950s, flamingo figurines were everywhere. Now flamingos are back in style!

The porcelain pheasants and bisque Tomtit and Goldfinch are further examples of high quality OJ pieces that give our collectible an air of respectability.

*A flock of flamingos. **Top row**: An 8¼" H. mother and her baby, Mark #43; a 3½" x 4" planter. Mark #116. **Bottom row**: A salt and pepper set, 2¾" H., one has opened wings; a wall pocket decorated with water lily leaves, 6½" x 6½", Mark similar to #116; realistically colored planter, 5½" X 7", Mark #43.*

A regal pheasant and his mate sit among pink flowers. Highly glazed with vibrant colors. 4¼" x 4¼" x 3". Frank Travis collection.

*These two birds perched on a branch are identified on the bottom
as being a Tomtit and a Goldfinch. See below for mark. The piece
is 5⅛″ W. and 2½″ H. Frank Travis collection.*

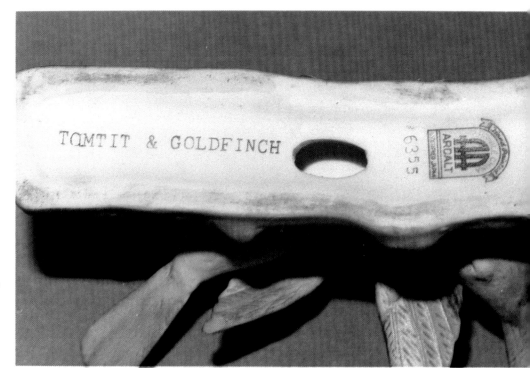

*The bottom of the bisque piece
shown above provides us with the
name of the birds and a good
view of the mark. Frank Travis
collection.*

Wall Plaques and Wall Pockets

Among the numerous items made to hang on our walls were some very fine bisque pieces and porcelain plaques.

Tiles could also be hung on the wall and those with dramatic colors demonstrate what could be attained in glazed porcelain.

Opposite page:
This 8" H. planter can either stand or be hung on the wall. This design was made in several variations. See page 138. Josephine Stine collection.

Interesting group of wall hangings. **Clockwise:** *An Oriental wall pocket featuring a ferocious-looking Siamese dancer, 6¾" H. with opening on top and bluish-green MIOJ; plaster-like Dutch girl plaque, 5¼" H. marked Yamska MIOJ in maroon; she has a mate somewhere. Highly glazed ceramic girl holding her doll, opening across the top of her hat, 9½" H. with Mark #4. A 6" H. lady in full skirted gown holding a basket of flowers on her hip has an opening in the upper back of her skirt. Unusual log cabin with fir tree on right rear. It has two openings on the back. A small square above a larger half circle. Could it be an incense burner? 4" H.*

A pair of three-dimensional bisque wall plaques. 10" x 12½". The boy is reading a letter, perhaps a love letter from the girl? These two pieces have exceptional detail. Mark #4. Frank Travis collection.

The 3¾" x 3¼" porcelain tile is decorated with fish and underwater plants in relief. Frank Travis collection.

This 5" H. porcelain wall pocket of a lady with a cloche hat reminds us of the 1920s Art Deco days. Frank Travis collection.

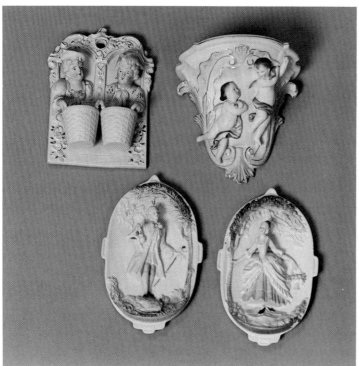

*These bisque wall plaques are of the quality which were sold in the finer gift shops. **Top row**: A boy and a girl leaning out a window with two baskets. 6¾" H. x 4¼" W. Mark #15. A plaque which also can serve as a shelf is decorated with two angels wearing pink and blue loin-clothes. 5¼" H. The shelf measures 5½" deep at its widest point. Mark #4. **Bottom row**: A Colonial man and woman in relief. 7" H. x 4⅜" W. This is a fairly common pair.*

Lamps and Candelabras

Lamps and lamp parts were a plentiful commodity during the Occupation. Many of the parts were shipped to the United States to be assembled into lighting fixtures there. It seems apparent that some of the assembly was never completed and we find that many of the statues (particularly bisque) in today's collections were intended for lamp decorations. Sometimes they are referred to as candle holders, but I believe this is an erroneous assumption.

Many of the bisque lamps were to be used as boudoir lamps, as were the porcelain colonial-figured ones.

Pair of beautiful boudoir lamps. The bisque figures stand 11½" H. Mark #4. I have seen pictures of these with the figurines placed on brass stands. They were referred to as boy and girl lamps and said to be rare. It is my opinion that they portray Little BoPeep and Little Boy Blue.

Three pair of bisque lamp bases. They are all approximately 10¼" H. The first pair are a smaller version of the pair above. The second boy and girl are attired in more formal dress. The gentleman and his lady wear 17th century garb. Frank Travis collection.

Lamps with decal copies of a Sevres decoration are of a more formal nature and would be more at home in the living room. The ruffled shades on lamps suggest that they were intended for the bedroom.

Many times we come across pieces on lamp bases that we believe are marked Made in Occupied Japan, but unless the dealer allows us to remove them from their bases, it is not a good idea to take a chance...unless, of course, the price is really cheap. Then the worst that can happen is that you would have a nice pair of lamps.

A pair of Sevres-type formal lamps decorated with a decal. The porcelain bases are 7½" H.

One of the largest pair of lamps I have seen. The porcelain bases measure 17" H. The base is 6½" in diameter. They are decorated with green medallions featuring gold trim and flowers. The mark is also one I haven't seen before. See below. These would be a nice addition to anyone's living room. Courtesy of Jack Woodmansee.

This unusual mark is found on the bottom of the large lamps pictured above.

These two candelabra are so overdone they are amusing! It seems as though the Japanese manufacturer tried to include everything he could think of in these two pieces. They have Mark #4; a mark which appears on many of the better pieces. 4½" H. figures of a boy and a girl stand on the bases. Above their heads in the center of the three arms of the candelabra stand identical 3¾" H. angels holding out their skirts. The candle holders have leaves beneath them.

The reverse sides astound us with their figures of squirrels standing at the base of the trees holding an armful of nuts. The pieces are further embellished with applied flowers and leaves. Truly an exercise in overexuberance! Each piece stands 9½" H. The cups with their leaves are attached to the three branches with metal nuts and bolts.

A lovely pair of boudoir lamps decorated with bluebonnets in relief and wearing their original shades. They measure 12¼" to the top of the socket. Frank Travis collection.

Silverplated candlesticks are among the few items made of that material.

A pair of shiny 3" H. metal candlesticks. The bases have a three ring design and are 3" round. The candleholders measure 2" round. They are marked Silverplated MIOJ. Art Gill collection.

Bottles

When I first found one of these figural bottles, (the cat and her kittens), I was puzzled as to what they were used for. From their corks I knew they had held some sort of liquid, but from the density and weight of the porcelain I was pretty sure that they had not held cologne.

Later I found the two dogs and puppies. One had a paper label on it which provided some answers. It read, "GUEST HOUSE CALIFORNIA PORT WINE Alcohol 19-21% by Vol. Bottled by Ron Virgin Co.,Ltd., Cambridge, Mass. Cap. 2 oz."

Still later, I discovered the Mexican bottle which had never been opened and whose contents still sloshed when shaken. It has a label on the front reading "RON VIRGIN RUM" and was bottled by the same company. This bottle holds 1.6 oz.

Six porcelain spirits bottles with corks. **Top row**: *The man playing the accordian measures 4½" H. A label on the back reads Prepared and Bottled by RON VIRGIN CO. LTD., CAMBRIDGE, MASS. Distributed by JOHN J. MINER & SONS, LTD. New York, N.Y. The Mexican still has his contents and stands 5¾" H. and is labeled RON VIRGIN RUM at feet. Another label on side reads: IMPORTED RUM 86 Proof Prepared and Bottled by RON VIRGIN CO. LTD. W.I.21 Cambridge, Mass. R:94 Contents 1.6 oz. The tennis player is 3¾" H.* **Bottom row**: *The 3¼" H. dog on left is empty and has a label which reads: GUEST HOUSE CALIFORNIA PORT WINE Alcohol 19-21% by Vol. Bottled by Ron Virgin Co.Ltd., Cambridge, Mass. Cap. 2oz. The cat with kitten is 2¼" high. The 3¼" H. dog on right also retains his contents but there is no label to tell us what they are.*

Eventually two more bottles came to light. The Accordion Player also has a label telling us that the contents were prepared and bottled by the Ron Virgin Co in Cambridge, Mass., but it also states that it was distributed by John J. Miner & Sons, Ltd. of New York City.

The Skeleton bottle is a bit grotesque but nonetheless interesting. Maybe the Japanese were trying to tell us that alcohol was detrimental to our health when they incised "poison" on the front of the bottle. I have seen pictures of this same bottle where the letters were outlined in the same gold as the crosses. Whoever painted my bottle may have neglected to finish the job.

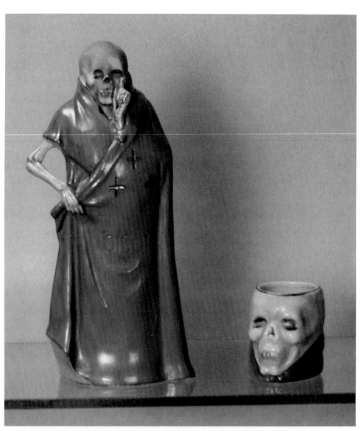

Skeleton liqueur set. Complete set has six shot glasses. Bottle is 6¾" H. Shot glass, 1¾" H.; embossed on front of robe is POISON.

Porcelain parrot bottle. 4¼" H. Frank Travis collection.

Two more figural liqueur bottles. The squirrel holding a jug is 3¾" H. Another cat and kitten with the kitten lying on top of the mother cat. The adult tiger cat has quite expressive eyes. It is 2½" H. with a 3¼" W. base. Both bottles like the ones shown on page 145 have the same black MIOJ stamp.

Perfume bottles are another highly sought-after OJ collectible. As so often happens in any collectible there is an overlap into other collectibles and currently perfume bottles are very popular, regardless of who made them. All of these bottles are embossed on the bottoms MIOJ. There were probably some whose paper labels have been lost. Another casualty of usage was the breakage of the daubers. Lucky is the collector who can find one that is not broken.

The porcelain bottle is interesting in that I have seen another label exactly like Mark #33 on a glass bottle except that it read, "Made in Czechoslovakia." The importer must have specialized in perfume bottles.

Perfume bottles are highly sought-after additions to any OJ collection. Fortunately most of the glass ones were embossed MIOJ on the bottoms. There are probably others which have lost their paper labels. **Top row**: *Crystal with rubber atomizer, 3¾" H.; pink, 3½" H.; pink, 3" H. blue, 3" H.* **Bottom row**: *3¼" H. pink bottle with dauber intact; pink and green with crosshatch pattern, 2¾" H.; 3⅞" H. green; ceramic perfume with rose topped stopper has round paper label Mark #33. I recently saw this same label on another glass perfume but it read, "Made in Czechoslovakia." The blue and pink bottles are 3½" H. All these glass bottles are embossed MIOJ on the bottoms.*

These 7½" H. porcelain cologne bottles with their rose decoration would make an attractive addition to any lady's dressing table. Mark #81. Frank Travis collection.

A three piece porcelain dresser set. The cologne bottles measure 4⅛" H. including the stoppers. Frank Travis collection.

Smoking Accessories

Once upon a time smoking was not deemed as dangerous to your health as it is today, and the Japanese took advantage of the fact that millions of Americans were addicted to the habit.

Hundreds of porcelain ashtrays and cigarette sets were imported. Many of the small trays fit inside the boxes. They were decorated with roses or similar flowers.

A group of smoking accessories. **Top row**: *A footed cigarette box decorated with moss roses, 2" H., 3¾" W. and 2½" deep; two-piece porcelain cigarette lighter, with a rose applied to the top. This lighter also comes in blue, 3¼" H.; a 3¼" x 4" pink ashtray with applied rose, probably had a box to match.* **Bottom row**: *The tray to this box stores inside. Again applied roses...this type of decoration is hard to find in mint condition since it chipped so easily. The box is 2" H., 4½" W. and 3½" deep and the ashtray is 2¾" x 3⅝"; a box and tray with moss rose decal decoration, the box is 1½" H., 4½" W. and 3" deep while the freeform tray is 3½" square; in the foreground is a 3½" diameter ashtray.*

Toby lighters are at the other end of the spectrum with their grotesque features. The metal inserts were incised with MIOJ. It is not too often that we find the Tobies marked.

Whimsical porcelain ashtrays can be used as candy dishes if you live in a non-smoking household. They would be delightful additions to any collection.

Porcelain Toby lighters. These two grotesque heads can be separated from their metal lighter inserts. They are 3¾" H. and are incised MIOJ on the bottom of the inserts. Art Gill collection.

A seated elf on a lily pad makes up this porcelain ashtray. 4" x 5". Mark #86. Frank Travis collection.

A humanoid porcelain ashtray with the figure of a girl bunny pointing to where she wants the ashes deposited. 4¼" x 4¼". Frank Travis collection.

Figural ashtrays are so exaggerated that they become humorous. They nearly make you want to light up just to see the smoke come out of their nostrils!

Some of the porcelain ashtrays would be at home in a collection of advertising memorabilia as well as OJ.

A pair of figural porcelain ashtrays are a bit silly. Both figures have bees sitting on their noses. One eye is closed while the other is fixed on the insect. The lady has a painted green beret on her head while the man wears a painted black skullcap. They have openings in their nostrils for the smoke to escape through. 3" H. x 4" W.

The front of this 2" H. and 5" round ceramic ashtray reads GUCKENHEIMER. Art Gill collection.

Metal smoking accessories flooded the market and many of the figural cigarette lighters are fun and easy to find. Animals were a popular subject but ship and camera lighters were unusual.

The reverse of the ceramic ashtray reads The American Distilling Company's. Not only an OJ collectible but a nice advertising collectible as well. Art Gill collection.

Back row: *Table top lighter can be changed into a pocket lighter by removing the base. 2½" H. x 2" W. Marked CORONA CONTINENTAL NEW YORK MIOJ. Camera lighter on a tripod. 4" H. x 2" W. Oversized lighter is 4" H. x 3" W. Marked RELIANCE MIOJ.* **Front row:** *A 3" long cylinder windproof lighter. Belt buckle lighter is 1" H. x 1¾" W. Zippo-like lighter with horse head decoration. 2¼" H. x 1½" W. Marked Continental, N.Y.*

A novel lighter in the shape of a table lamp. 4½" H. x 3" W. Pulling on the cord causes the lighter to light. The piano lighter is 2½" H. x 2½" W. x 3" deep when closed. Art Gill collection.

Metal figural lighters. **Top row:** *Dog with hydrant, 3" H. x 2" W., marked MIOJ with a K under a set of wings; an elephant with a howdah and his trunk up for good luck, 3" H. x 3½" W.; a camel, 3" H. x 3½" W., marked camel with YK, MIOJ.* **Bottom row:** *Arabian horse, 4½" x 4¼", marked same as camel; swan, 2" H. x 3" W., marked T-MIOJ; a horse's head, 3¼" H. x 3" W., marked with a Y in a diamond, MIOJ. Art Gill collection.*

Three interesting metal lighters. Ship with original box. Box measures 2" H. x 5" W. Porter "Lift it Lights", 4½" H. x 3½" W.; pot belly stove, 3½" H. x 2½" W. Art Gill collection.

An assortment of metal lighters. **Back row:** *The woman figural lighter is 3¼" H. and 2¼" W.; the horse head is 3⅜" H. and 3⅛" W.* **Center Row:** *The Aladdin's lamp lighter is 2¾" H. on a 5½" W. tray. The cowboy boot is 2⅞" H.; the smaller horse head is 2⅞" H. and 2⅜" W.* **Front:** *The boat lighter is 1⅞" H. and 4¾" W. Frank Travis collection.*

Baskets

One little-known area of collecting Occupied Japan items is that of baskets which the Japanese made both in bamboo and willow. They include fishing creels, pocketbooks, picnic baskets, sewing baskets, Easter baskets, flower baskets...just about every kind of utility basket imaginable. However, OJ baskets are not easy to find. While many are stamped with a purple MIOJ stamp, others were sold with paper stickers and, as we all know, paper labels have a way of becoming lost. It is quite possible that some of the older baskets found at flea markets started life in Occupied Japan.

Much of the workmanship in OJ baskets is of high quality. Two-handled baskets could have held flowers or perhaps an arrangement of fruit. Fishing creels are decorated with leather strips, while small Easter baskets are very similar to those we use today.

Dark baskets are sometimes marked in white. For every OJ basket picked up at a flea market, two or three will be found not marked...but there is always that possibility that one will be!

A square sewing basket with a handle on cover. It has a tufted pink satin lining. In mint condition. Measures 8¼" square and 6" high. Marked with purple MIOJ stamp.

Flower basket has a paper label MIOJ and is 15" x 10" x 4½". The fishing creel stands 8¼" high and is 14" in width, stamped MIOJ. The small Easter basket stands 4¾" H. to the top of the handle, stamped MIOJ in purple. Margaret Bolbat collection.

Basket on the left folds flat to measure 15" x 10" x 1". The other basket measures 5¾" x 5½" x 5½". Both stamped MIOJ. Margaret Bolbat collection.

A two-tiered sewing basket, 8½" x 6" x 6⅜" with a black MIOJ stamped on the bottom twice. **Top right:** 6¾" x 5" x 4" basket, stamped twice with MIOJ. **Bottom right:** a 6½" x 9½" x 3¾" basket with a purple MIOJ stamped on the bottom. Margaret Bolbat collection

Celluloid

It is a miracle that so many celluloid pieces marked Made in Occupied Japan remain today. The material is very fragile and most of the pieces were made as children's toys and dolls. Celluloid is a tough, flammable thermoplastic which was not a good choice for children's playthings.

Today it is difficult to find dolls in mint condition. Their movable arms were attached with slender elastic and through the years these pieces have become stretched causing the arms to hang away from their sockets.

Nevertheless, there are still plenty of celluloid pieces waiting to be discovered. Kewpie dolls and the carnival dolls with their feathered costumes are highly desirable additions to an OJ collection. Some of the nude dolls were purchased for the express purpose of being dressed by indulgent grandmothers and many wear handmade crocheted outfits and lace outfits.

Three celluloid carnival dolls in their feathered finery. These usually came affixed to a stick and were offered as prizes in games of chance at carnivals and beaches. They are 7", 8½" and 11½" in height. Marked on their backs. Art Gill collection.

A 5¾" H. celluloid blue policeman holds a billy club. Two celluloid girls with lace dresses, both 4" H. One stands while the other sits. A 5" H. nude baby. All have embossed marks on backs. Art Gill collection.

A lineup of seven celluloid dolls ranging in size from 5" to 7½" H. All have movable arms except for the center girl drying dishes. Marked on backs. Art Gill collection.

Search among your Christmas decorations for the Rudolph the Red-nosed Reindeer. Members of the OJ club tell stories of discovering that they unknowingly had one which was unpacked every year and never examined it to see if it was marked MIOJ. A herd of reindeer also served as Christmas decorations.

More celluloid figures include a 7" H. stork and a 6¾" H. Rudolph the Red Nosed Reindeer. The two colorful swans are 3½" and 4" long. The Indian is 2" H. seated in a 3½" long canoe. Art Gill collection.

*A herd of five celluloid reindeer ranging in size from 2¾" to 7" H.
All have magnificent antlers and are marked MIOJ on their
stomachs. Art Gill collection.*

Baby rattles were made but not too many have survived. The nodders are hard to find in good condition. Their heads are easily separated from their bodies and the constant nodding had an effect on their longevity.

On the left stands a 7½" H. celluloid doll with movable arms and gold painted air. **Top row**: *A 2¼" H. x 3¼" W. swan; a 2½" H. x 4¼" W. (to the tip of his tail) lion; a 2" H. x 2¾" W. rhinoceros and a 2½" H. x 3¼" W. hippopotamus.* **Bottom row**: *A nodding donkey, 3¾"H. x 4¾" W.; a 3" H. mini celluloid doll; a baby in bunting rattle with a blue handle, 7½" long, embossed MIOJ on back of handle and back of baby's neck.*

Five celluloid animal nodders. The two elephants measure 4" H. and 2¾" H. The donkeys are 3", 3½" and 5½" H. These are called nodders because a slight touch to their heads causes them to nod. Embossed on stomachs. Art Gill collection.

Most of the celluloid pieces have the MIOJ mark embossed. Occasionally the mark is faint so that if you don't know where to look, it can be overlooked.

A large variety of celluloid articles were manufactured and exported to the United States. Now they would be considered too dangerous for a child to play with.

Three seated celluloid babies. Baby in yellow outfit is 5½" H. The naked baby is 7" H. while the doll in the red bunting is 8" H. All are embossed MIOJ on their backs. Art Gill collection.

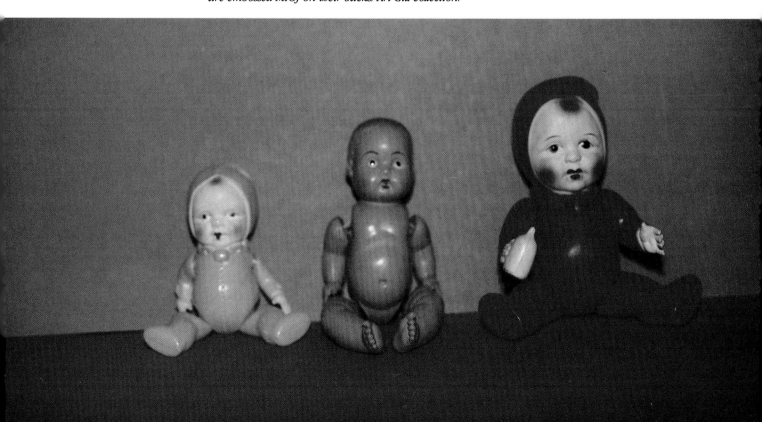

Celluloid sports figures. Three football players ranging in size from 4" to 6" H. All carry footballs. A 4½" H. baseball player prepares to bat. Marked on backs. Art Gill collection.

Two 5½" high celluloid boys wearing blue shorts and red polka-dotted ties flank a pair of 2¾" high celluloid Dutch children. The boy and girl were purchased in their original box. MIOJ on backs. Art Gill collection.

This bunch of celluloid animals are very realistically done except for their colors. I have never seen a purple gorilla or a white lion. They range in size from 1¾" to 3¾" H. **Top row**: *Tiger, rhinoceros, bulldog, and lion.* **Bottom row**: *A saddled horse, gazelle, giraffe and that purple gorilla. Marked MIOJ on backs. Art Gill collection.*

These two blue celluloid bears with pink bow ties are 4" and 6" H. The pink bear stands 3¾" H. All have embossed marks on back. Art Gill collection.

Two Roly-Poly celluloid dolls with weighted bottoms. The larger is 6" H. and dings when it is rocked. The small one measures 3½" H. Art Gill collection.

These dolls range in size from 3½" to 5" H. and are all marked on their backs. No. 2 Kewpie doll is highly sought after by both doll collectors and OJ collectors. No. 3 holds a baby bottle. Art Gill collection.

Clocks

OJ clocks took many shapes and forms and included wall clocks, mantel clocks and alarm clocks.

The birdcage clock has to be one of the most splendid items. It is hard to find a complete one since it was comprised of many different parts.

Some porcelain pieces were made to be assembled into clocks when they reached this country, such as an 8″ case decorated with flowers and cherubs that contains a movement marked Sessions.

A clock with a wooden case has a pendulum and is marked EIKEISHA on the dial. Alarm clocks were made of metal and were footed.

In 1949, a Japanese Trade Guide was issued in an effort to stimulate the exportation of goods and contains a lot of good information. For example, it states that during the year ending June, 1947, there were approximately 170,000 watches and clocks exported to Hong Kong, Singapore, the Netherlands East Indies and the United States, in that order. This, however, does not give a clue as to how many were exported to the US.

Clocks marked with the POPPO logo of the Tezuka Clock Co.,Ltd., the trade guide states, were made by the Awano Mfg. Co., Ltd. of Tokyo. These pigeon springless clocks worked by chain, keep correct time.

A gold-like and chrome metal birdcage clock. It contains a bird below a round ball with numbers that serve as the face of the clock and is set on a marble-like base. There are MIOJ marks on the bottom of the cage, on the clock part and on the metal of the support. The numbered ball turns in the cage and the bird turns back and forth with each tick. With the stand the clock measures 8½″ H. The clock alone is 5½″ H. Art Gill collection.

A wonderful Betty Boop clock. Made of wood, the eyes move back and forth as the pendulum ticks. This clock also comes with black hair. It is 13″ H. and measures 6¼″ at its widest part. Marked POPPO. MIOJ under numeral six.

A heavy metal pine cone weight runs the clock, and when they tick, the eyes on the figures move back and forth. Other figural clocks made by this company include a Betty Boop with dark hair, a dog, a baseball player, a cat and a teddy bear. Instructions to work these clocks leave a lot to be desired:

How to handle the Clock

This clock moves by pulling down the left edge chain, and draw a weight once a day. It is right place to hang this that as you can hear balanced sound of tick of the movement when you got the right position, please fix this by against to the pillar with the nail, which there is the back of the case; If on the case of go too fast, you may pull down the weight, and go slow it, you may draw up the weight, so this clock keep the right time. If you to be correctly the time, you may turn the long hand, This hand, is free to turn left or right

MANUFACTURER TEZUKA CLOCK CO., LTD.

Honestly, this is exactly how the label on the back of one of these clocks reads!

This wonderful wooden owl clock was manufactured by the same company as the Betty Boop clock on the previous page and is marked the same. It has a rich deeply carved exterior. 10" H. and 6" W. The eyes on this one also move back and forth while it ticks. Art Gill collection.

Another clock by the Tezyka Clock Co., Ltd. This one copies the German Black Forest cuckoo clocks in every detail. It is 17" H. x 13" W. It is run with acorn weights, and cuckoos; that is, if you don't let it run down because it drives you cuckoo! Art Gill collection.

A closeup of the cuckoo clock at left shows the MIOJ under the Roman numeral VI and the POPPA Clock logo. Art Gill collection.

A Mixture of Metal

MIOJ metal objects are not difficult to find today, yet it is difficult to find the metal in good condition. The majority of these pieces were stamped from a hard, brittle material called antimony and they have not held up well.

Many were intended for the tourist trade and are stamped with the name of a resort or vacation spot. There are many novelty items which fall into this category. The little girls who loved horses had a choice of statues for their collections.

Metal cowboy hat measuring 1½" H. x 3½" W., marked MIOJ on the rim. A Samuri helmet with beautiful detail measuring 2" H. x 2¾" in diameter. Art Gill collection.

A 4" round metal ship's wheel ashtray. The souvenir of someone's trip to the Statue of Liberty. Frank Travis collection.

A metal ashtray featuring the Empire State Building marked CMC Ware. 3" H. x 5" W. x 3¼" deep. A metal replica of St. Peter's Basilica. 3" H. x 1¾" W. x 3½" deep. Art Gill collection.

Four metal animals: A 2" x 2" saddle horse; a 2¼" H. x 2½" W. prospector's mule; a similar mule has a decal proclaiming it a souvenir of the St. Louis Zoo; a 1¼" H. x 2½" W. polar bear is marked with the bird SNF MIOJ mark. Art Gill collection.

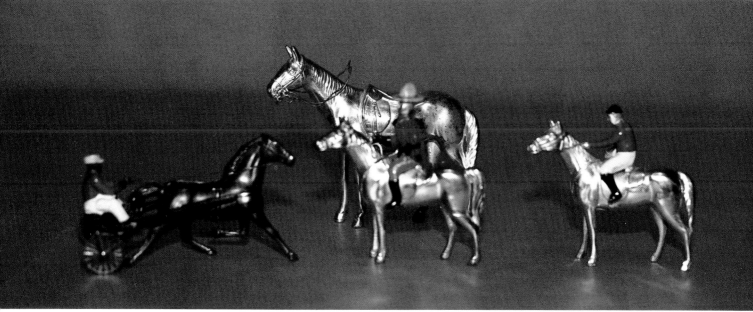

Four metal horse statues. The 2½" H. x 5" W. harness racer has a black driver. The saddled horse in the rear measures 4½" H. x 5¼" W. In front of him a Royal Canadian Mounted Policeman sits on his mount. 4" H. x 3¾" W. A jockey prepares to take his horse to the gate, 3½" H. by 3¾" W. All bear the camel with YK MIOJ mark. Art Gill collection.

Boxes were popular and some were very attractive, being enhanced with enamel decoration.

Combination piano music and cigarette box with blue enameled decoration. 3½" H. x 5" W. x 8" deep. Dragons against a red enameled background decorate this jewelry jox lined with orange corduroy-like fabric. 2½" H. x 6¾" W. x 4" deep. Art Gill collection.

Metal footed money box with key. The top is decorated with a ship and treasure bags against a deep blue enameled background with a dragon motif along the edges. The sides show replicas of Japanese coins. 2" H. x 5" W. x 4" deep. Art Gill collection.

Opposite page top:

Some examples of decorative metal. Most of the metal used was antimony and the plating has not held up well. **Top row**: *A 3" x 5" covered cigarette box with embossed mark; three nut dishes with a pierced border. The scene in the center shows three angels, one playing a violin, with a church in the background, embossed mark, 4" x 5½". The finish on these is like new.* **Middle row**: *A 2½" H. metal lighter on a 3⅛" x 5" tray that doubles as an ashtray, both marked with embossed MIOJ; two-handled vase with an open peony in relief, 7¾" H., marked MIOJ HKK in a diamond; pink silk-lined footed jewelry casket shaped like a crown. Embossed MIOJ with earth with wings logo. Also has Coney Island decal. 3" W. x 2¼" deep.* **Bottom row**: *Round covered dish with floral design. Flower inside cover. 4¼" in diameter, dish 1¼" deep; cigarette lighter, both pieces marked PKS in diamond MIOJ, 2" H.; Stand up picture frame featuring pagoda with dragon design. Artist signed in bottom of right pillar, NIKKO. MIOJ in right corner of frame, 6⅝"x 9½" with flowers enameled in red and leaves in green.*

Opposite page bottom:

Two metal picture frames. The pagoda frame is 8⅝" H. and 7⅛" W. with a 3½" x 5½" opening. The mark is embossed on the inside of the frame and can only be found if the back and the picture are removed. The smaller frame is 3⅜" x 4⅜". The design edge is ¾" W.. The glass under the design is painted a rusty red. The mark MIOJ is on a little extra tab on the back of the frame. Margaret Bolbat collection.

Some utilitarian items were also made. Bookends, pencils, picture frames, and other pieces served a useful as well as decorative function.

Two metal animals with attached 3" long mechanical pencils with their original marked boxes. Art Gill Collection.

This pair of bookends has a copper look over a white metal. 5¾" H. The ships are separate pieces with an embossed MIOJ. A nut and bolt fastens them to the base. The bases are encised MIOJ. Margaret Bolbat collection.

Miniature cocktail shakers, and glasses, shot glasses, and eggs are other metal items marked "Made in Occupied Japan".

The Seven Gods of Good Luck are one of the few themes made for the American market that reflect the Japanese culture. They would be an interesting and appropriate part of any collection.

A most unusual item is the key to the City of Los Angeles decorated with scenes of the city. One wonders how many other cities had these keys.

Two examples of some of the metal miniatures produced during the occupation. A cocktail shaker with tray and four glasses. The tray is 3" in diameter and incised MIOJ, the shaker is 2½" H. and incised Japan while the 1" H. glasses are unmarked. There could have been six glasses originally as there is room on the tray for them. The four 1½" H. shot glasses fit inside the chrome egg and are incised MIOJ. The egg is marked RELIANCE CHICAGO MIOJ and is 2⅜" H.

The Seven Gods of Good Luck. These seven figures are numbered, left to right, one through seven. Only the figures with numbers 1 & 2 are marked MIOJ. They range from 2" to 2¼" in height and measure an average of 1¼" in diameter. No. 1 is Ebisu, the God of Food. He holds a fishing pole in his right hand and a large fish in his left. No. 2 is Diakoku, the God of Wealth. He holds a magical hammer in his right hand, strands of two rice bags and has a bag of rice thrown over his left shoulder. No. 3 is Bishamon, the God of Glory. He holds a spear in his right hand and a pagoda in his left. No. 4 is Hotei, the God of Contentment, the best known of all the Gods and probably the most copied. He carries a fan in his left hand and a bag of rice thrown over his right shoulder. No. 5 is Fukurohuju, the God of Success. He has a long beard and carries a scroll in his right hand while a swan sits by his left knee. No. 6 is Jurojin, the God of Long Life. There is the head of a stag in front of his right side. No. 7 is Bentin, the God of Beauty and Charity. The only female of the Seven Gods, she is playing a Biwa (Samisen) and is the patron of the arts -Music and Literature. The Seven Gods are made of a bronze-like metal and were originally shipped in wooden boxes with Japanese writing. Art Gill collection. (Research by Robert W. Gee, Jr.)

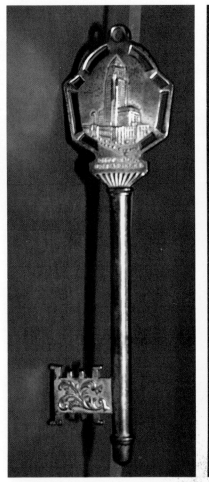 

A metal key to the city of Los Angeles. The frontside shows City Hall. 7¼" long. Art Gill collection.

The reverse side of the key to the city of Los Angeles pictures the Public Library. The mark can be read on the bottom protrusion.

Wood and Papier Maché

No collection of OJ would be complete without some wooden items. Many of these have the appearance of inlaid surfaces. Some were manufactured to serve purely as decorative items while others had a function. For example, a tiny tea set contained in the wooden apple was a nice present to bring a little person from a trip.

Back row: Wooden doll's dresser or jewelry box, 5½" H. x 4" W. x 2¼" deep, with a typical Japanese landscape. A cigarette dispenser, side view on page 170, an intricately inlaid box with flowers inside cover. Another cigarette dispenser. This one measures 2½" H. x 3½" W. x 2¾" deep. Front row: Two wooden rickshaws being pulled by rickshaw boys and carrying Japanese ladies with parasols. 3" H. x 3½" W. All are stamped MIOJ on the bottom. Art Gill collection.

The front of a pair of paper wrapped wooden chopsticks packaged for the Miyako Restaurant at 20 West 56th St. in New York City. Art Gill collection.

The reverse side of the 8½" long chopsticks. Art Gill collection.

Back row: A clicker party noisemaker, 6" long; a box containing seven coasters with a rose design is 2¼" H. and 3¾" round. The coasters also have a rose on them. Front row: Two 6" long carved wooden letter openers; a wooden salad fork and spoon measuring 10" long and incised MIOJ. Art Gill collection.

This 2½" H. yellow wooden apple opens to reveal that it contains a set of miniature wooden dishes consisting of a coffee pot, two cups and saucers and a bowl. Each piece is decorated with a red apple. Frank Travis collection.

Of a more utilitarian nature is the rolling pin. Papier maché dishes and trays were advertised as being alcohol proof, even though some show damage from water spotting.

Other wooden items include salad bowl sets, carpenter's rulers, pianos, china cabinets, slide rules, captain's chairs, drop leaf tables, children's puzzles, and some carved figurines. There is also a folding bamboo hosiery drier composed of two slats of wood forming an "X", with a hanger at the top and four or eight spring-type clothespins hanging from it.

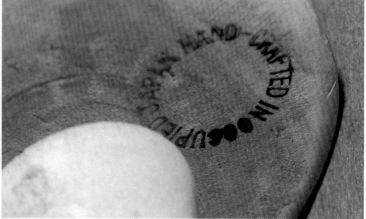

The mark on the rolling pin pictured at left is stamped on the end by the handle and informs us that this piece was handcrafted. Frank Travis collection.

One of the many utilitarian items manufactured by the Japanese was this wooden rolling pin. It is full-sized at 17" in length. Frank Travis collection.

*A selection of wooden and papier maché items. **Top row**: A 10½" x 12" papier maché tray with a red K in circle MIOJ mark; a 9½" papier maché plate. **Middle row**: 5¼" round hand painted plate with oriental scene; an ivory-like parade of elephants over a bridge. The black wooden base measures 6¼" W. MIOJ embossed on back of bridge; a 4" H. wooden ship on a 4" W. base. **Bottom row**: When the top of this cigarette box is opened, a bird comes up with a cigarette clasped in his beak, outside of box is inlaid with a wooden design, stamped on bottom MIOJ with five rows of five numbers each, bottom row reads 89858. 4½" H. and 3¾" sq. Another view of this box appears on previous page. Three drawer chest is 3⅛" H. x 4¼" W. x 2⅜" deep. The tops and sides are decorated with an inlaid pattern and the front has painted flowers on it.*

Cameras, Microscopes and Binoculars

Men are more apt to add these to their collections.

The Japanese have long had a knack for manufacturing cameras. The same names we recognize today, Canon, Minolta and Olympus, show up on the OJ cameras. These are real mini-cameras and all come with their own carrying cases.

Three 16 MM miniature cameras all marked MIOJ with their carrying cases. All are 2½" long. Frank Travis collection.

A group of cameras all marked Made in Occupied Japan. **Top row**: *Canon Serenar F.4 100 MM lens; Minolta 35 Model F; Mamiya 16.* **Bottom row**: *Second camera, Stecky Subminiature Camera; Canon Wide Angle Serenar 35 MM F 3.5 lens; Olympus Zuiko 1.2.8 F 40M lens; Mighty Camera. Margaret Bolbat collection.*

A miniature microscope clearly shows the stamp on the wooden box which houses it.

Binoculars in all sizes and with many different powers can be found. Most of the markings are found on the screws which adjust the range.

A 4½″ H. miniature microscope with wooden box. Marked BOBBY 80X MIOJ with a paper label. The 5″ H. box is stamped MIOJ. Art Gill collection.

*Four sets of binoculars in varying sizes along with a metal telescope. **Back row:** No. 1 has 7 x 50 power; No. 2, 6 x 25 power. **Front row:** No. 1, 6 x 15 power and No. 3 has 3 power. The telescope is 3 power. Art Gill collection.*

This pair of binoculars are 3½″ W. and a decal tells us that they are a souvenir of the Canadian side of Niagara Falls. Frank Travis collection.

Lacquerware

The manufacture of lacquerware during the occupation reached a new height of workmanship. Unfortunately, the American public was reluctant to believe the claims the Japanese made that a finish which looked so vulnerable was resistant to heat, alcohol and water.

Because of the long and involved process used in its manufacture, lacquerware had to sell for exorbitant prices.

Lacquerware is generally found marked in one of two ways. Most of the wood-based pieces were imported by Crockery Importers of Newington, Ct. and bear their rooster logo. We most often find Mark #51 on the metal-based items.

A brochure from Crockery Imports tells us that their lacquerware was "offered as one of Japan's finest examples of industrial arts. Behind its exotic charm and perfection of finish are the matchless skills and experience of five hundred years."

It took an average of twenty-six different steps and six man hours to make a piece of lacquerware. Most were made in the Japanese cottage industry since the factories had been destroyed. The piece was finished by painting it with a hard varnish made from the sap of the lacquer tree. Collectors are fortunate that the owners of these exquisite pieces were reluctant to put them to hard use.

A 10¼" H. and 10¼" W. lacquerware compote. The pedestal measures 6" high. Mark #51. Margaret Bolbat collection.

A lacquerware console set, planter is 8" long, 5⅛" W. and 5⅝" deep; the candlesticks measure 4½" H. on a 2⅝" W. base. The candle inserts are removable. Mark #51. Margaret Bolbat collection.

Crockery Imports dealt in wine glasses, tumblers, cups and saucers, jewel boxes, napkin rings, trays, plates and salad sets, just to mention a few.

Metal-based pieces were highly decorative as well. Many of the designs were enhanced with 24-karat gold dust. Whether you come upon a wood-based piece or a metal-based piece, you will surely have found an important addition to your collection.

An unusual shaped lacquerware bowl with metal base, decorated with irisdescent chips, Mark #51, 7½" W., 6" from front to back.

A representation of some of the finer lacquerware pieces made during the Occupation. The covered bowl is on a metal base and measures 5" x 5". Mark #51. The tumbler with the bird decoration is 5" H. and has the Crockery Imports logo; the second tumbler is 5⅝" H. and the peacock has mother of pearl imbedded in the tail. Mark #51. The cardholder is 5¼" H. Mark #51. Margaret Bolbat collection.

A set of six red wood lacquerware standard sized cups and saucers in original box. Inside of cups are gold and each cup has a different design. Marked MIOJ in gold. Margaret Bolbat collection.

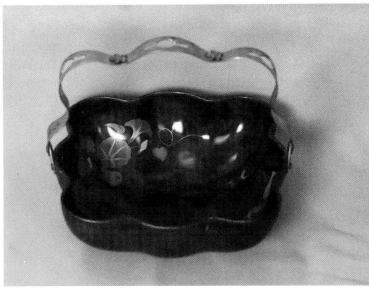

An 8" x 10" wall pocket with bamboo pattern. Marked with Maruni paper sticker and D558-1. Margaret Bolbat collection.

This lacquerware basket with a metal handle is decorated with blue morning glories. It is 7¼" square and measures 6½" to the top of the handle. Mark #51. Courtesy of Jean Henshaw.

This lovely 14½" W. lazy susan has a removable 7" W. center dish, it rotates on ball bearings housed in the 3" H. stand and is marked Made by Hand in Occupied Japan Maruni. Margaret Bolbat collection.

Salad bowl set, lacquerware on a wooden base. Large bowl is 13" round, individual bowls, 6". Marked Hand-Crafted Occupied Japan in a circle.

Sewing

Sewing machines were among the utilitarian items produced by the Japanese. Both cabinet types and portables were made. They were often identified by a metal plate attached to the machine. Others have been found marked Mercury (with the internal parts marked Toyota) and Simplex.

Another of the more utilitarian imports from Japan during the occupation consisted of a number of different makes of sewing machines. This is one of the many that have surfaced. A cabinet machine, it is 8¼" H. x 14½" W. x 7" deep and is marked with the plate shown at left. Frank Travis collection.

The 1½" x 1¾" plate affixed to the sewing machine pictured at right tells us that it is an Elite, manufactured by the Elite Sewing Machine Corp. and Made in US Occupied Japan. This is the first time I have seen US used before the OJ. Frank Travis collection.

Sewing notions were made for the dime stores. Needle packets are highly collectible, if only for the graphics. Some appear to have been left over from before the war.

Pincushions were sometimes part of sewing kits, or tufted fabric inserted into openings in ceramic figures. A cute little celluloid pig has a tape measure from his mouth and falls into the celluloid category, too.

Two of the more colorful needle packs found in the dime stores of the 40s and 50s. These have some colorful and attractive graphics. The first shows two kittens playing with a ball of yarn while two women are very interested in what one is knitting. The Army and Navy Needle Book shows a steam-driven naval vessel. Perhaps this lithograph was left over from before the war? Both are marked on the backs MIOJ. Frank Travis collection.

Some of the many sewing notions made during the Occupation. The sewing kits are identical except for the color of their pincushion tops. They hold six spools of thread and a gold-like thimble. MIOJ is impressed on their cardboard bottoms. They are 2½" in diameter. The label on the small needle pack reads Gotham Silver eyed Sharps 3/9 with MIOJ printed across the bottom. The white Army and Navy envelope holds the Diamond drilled eyed sharps in the package below.

A cute celluloid pig has a tape measure coming out of his mouth. 2⅜" W. The beginning of the tape is stamped Occupied Japan in large letters above a smaller MIOJ. Frank Travis collection.

We find buttons on cards and strung on thread. Other findings were braid, artificial flowers, hat bodies, and safety pins. The linen shirtings, and inter-linings and other fabrics available for export probably went to dress manufacturers.

This 8" x 3" x 3¾" cardboard box contains a dozen paper bags each marked Line 12 MIOJ. Inside each paper bag is a 16" long string of miniature crocheted buttons also marked with a cardboard tag. The box is marked No 243 MIOJ Line 12. Margaret Bolbat collection.

Jewelry, Scarves and Fans

Costume jewelry made during the occupation has become one of the more elusive items to find. Most of it was labeled with paper tags that were removed before the jewelry was worn.

A complete boxed set of jewelry may be marked on only one piece.

This box of tulip shaped jewelry is set with green stones. It consists of screwback earrings, a necklace, an expansion bracelet, and a brooch. We are told that it was from The Style Guild Collection. The bracelet is marked on one link but all the other pieces are unmarked. The box has a celluloid bottom and a cardboard cover. The same logo appears on the cover of the box. Art Gill collection. The 18" long three-strand pearl necklace has a paper label. The clasp is simply marked Japan.

Expansion bracelets are marked on one link. Bone china earring and pin sets with tiny flowers also exist, but the marks are hard to find unless you unglue them from their findings. Single and triple strands of pearls and glass beads may retain their paper labels.

Top row: *Necklace with metal medallion, marked T in a diamond MIOJ. A cowboy boot pin from the New York State Fair. Similar pins are shown on next page.* ***Bottom row:*** *Three expansion bracelets. Nos. 1 and 3 are the same except for the color of the stones and are marked DALE MIOJ. The center rhinestone bracelet is marked "Lady Patricia" MIOJ. Art Gill collection.*

Jewelry pins made of celluloid are not hard to find. A large quantity of Scottie dogs were discovered in a warehouse in 1986 and came on the market. A selection of other pins manufactured for the American trade included a pressed metal cowboy riding a horse.

Saturday matinee fans of cowboys of the day must have loved the novelty pins which included Hopalong Cassidy, The Lone Ranger, Roy Rogers, and Gene Autry.

Several silk scarves have come to light and they are just as fashionable today. One takes as an unusual subject, all the chickens of the world, and identifies some of them by name. They have the same sewn-in tag of their importer Baar and Beards, Inc.

These cowboy pins with red, white and blue ribbons and thinly stamped metal boots feature Hopalong Cassidy, The Lone Ranger and Roy Rogers. Have also seen Gene Autry. The boot is pinned to the ribbon and marked MIOJ on the pin back. There is an illegible imprint on the reverse of the pins. Perhaps they were manufactured in the States and assembled here. The pin is 1¼" in diameter and the boot is 2 3/16" long.

Five plastic pins ranging in size from 1" to 1¾". All marked MIOJ on their pin backs. A large number of these Scottie pins surfaced in 1986 after a warehouse find came on the market. They are very colorful. Art Gill collection.

A colorful 33" x 34" silk scarf picturing the chickens of the world, some of which include Heart Breaker, American Bantams and Black Bantams. Art Gill collection.

Four celluloid pins. A 1¾" round pin; a rectangular ivory-like carved flower pin, 1½" H. x 2¼" W.; a small ½" H. daisy pin on card stamped OJ; an openwork lacepin, 1¼" H. x 1⅛" W. All have incised MIOJ on their pin backs. Art Gill collection.

Pins. A 1½" H. metal cowboy roping a bull and a plastic pin with two elves and a Princess, 1½" H. x 1½" W., are incised MIOJ on their pin backs. A 2" round beaded baby's bracelet has a paper label. The 3½" cuckoo clockpin on cardboard is stamped MIOJ on the back of the card. Art Gill collection.

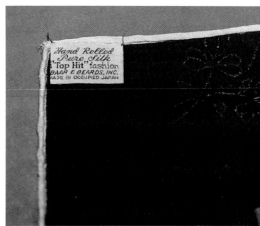

These three silk scarfs all have sewn-in labels which read: Handrolled, pure silk, Top Hit Fashion, Baar & Beard Inc, Made in Occupied Japan. The green one measures 32" x 32"; the pink and white, 12½" x 42" and the blue and yellow with Fleur de Lis is 28" long. Margaret Bolbat collection.

The sewn-in tags on the corners of the scarves at left and on page 179 tells us that they are HandRolled Pure Silk "Top Hit" Fashions from Baar and Beards Inc. and MIOJ.

It is not surprising that we find folding fans marked MIOJ. After all, the Japanese invented them. They were made of paper, or wooden slats, cloth and silk with lovely iridescent mother-of-pearl decoration on the ribs. Sometimes a fan is not marked, but the oilskin paper envelope which holds it is stamped MIOJ.

*The top fan has flowers handpainted on silk. Its beauty is enhanced by mother-of-pearl decoration and it has a metal loop with a tassel. MIOJ stamped on the spine. 8¼" x 15½" W. when opened. Bottom fan has printed across the top "PARADISE OF HAWAII" and is decorated with scenes of the islands. **Top row**: left to right: Surf Riders Waikiki Beach, Hibiscus Hawaii, Hilo Bay With Maunakea Mt. and Kilauea Volcano Hawaii National Park. **Bottom row**: Hula Dancers Hawaii, Kamehameha Statue, and Waikiki Beach Honolulu. The fan is paper with wooden slats and is not marked but its paper wrapper reads PARADISE OF HAWAII MADE IN OCCUPIED JAPAN.*

Toys and Dolls

Lucky are those of you who bought your OJ toys before the costs spiraled out of sight. A "Running Mickey on Pluto" that did have the MIOJ mark sold for $9,680 at a Christie's auction on March 28, 1990. There were a tremendous number of windup toys made during the Occupation and many can be found in their original boxes.

Dime store and novelty items are still around, but some of the rubber toys have hardened with age and others have become separated from their packaging.

A 4" H. windup Gentleman Frog toy with original box. His legs are tin and the rest of his body and hat and cane are celluloid. He is embossed MIOJ on his lower back. Margaret Bolbat collection.

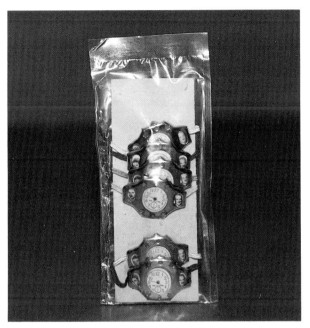

A cellophane wrapped package containing six children's play metal watches with elastic bands. The back of the card is marked MIOJ. Art Gill collection.

An assortment of children's novelty toys common to the dime store trade. 1. 5" H. gun and holster set. 2. 7" long all rubber hatchet. 3. 5¼" long rubber knife with sheath. 4, 5, and 6 are rubber water squirters. The snake is 4¼" long, the dog with the celluloid head is 3¾" long and the camera is 1½" H. 7. A 5½" long metal water pistol. 8. A rubber cigar with a cigar ring reading HAVANA. squeeze it and a snake comes out. The rubber on the squirters, as so often happens, has hardened with age. Art Gill collection.

These children's toys were often found in the dime and variety stores and probably none of them cost over 50 cents. The Dolls Nursing Set includes a baby bottle and a rattle. The box is 3½" x 2½" and is marked across the lower front. The second box contains a duck which when squeezed whistles. Box measures 1½" x 2½". The magnet on its original card is 2½" H. and is marked on the bottom of the card. The cat and mouse game is 2" in circumference. The kaleidoscope is 4½" long amd decorated with a lady pig. Art Gill collection.

Doll and children's tea sets were plentiful, and complete sets marked MIOJ are bringing good prices. Here is another instance where only parts of the sets are marked and quite often if the box is lost you have no way to substantiate the age of the dishes. Single dishes are plentiful but unless you find a boxed set it is difficult to find a complete one.

Some miniature and child's tea sets. **Top row**: *Mini-set on a three-tiered wood stand, pot, 2¼" H., the creamer is 1½" H., two cups and saucers and no sugar bowl! The stand is stamped with a purple MIOJ and all the porcelain pieces are marked merely Japan; six 3¾" child's Blue Willow dinner plates and a 5" wide soup tureen, all marked MIOJ in blue.* **Middle row**: *Toy Tea Set with original box and packing excelsior, lusterware pot, sugar and creamer and two cups and saucers. Decorated with a flower decal. The pot stands 2¼" H. The label on top of box is marked and a narrow label on the side reads "No. 599 TOYTEASET Made in Occupied Japan"; mini tea set on a 3" W. tray, tray marked PICO MIOJ, other pieces not marked; 2" H. footed pot; 1¾" H. mini pot (probably part of a set) marked with a rectangle in a square and a line drawn through; pink mini teaset on 3½" round tray, two cups and saucers, creamer and sugar, and pot. Tray marked MIOJ, box marked No. 4711 MIOJ with purple stamp.* **Bottom row**: *Hexagon shaped flowered tea cup with gold handle, saucer 2⅞" W., rectangle in a circle mark; 1¼" H. scallop-edged cup with Florida scene featuring palm trees, saucer is 2¾" W., marked Burger, Miami Handpainted OJ in red; green mini teaset, same as pink above; 1¾" H. cup with 3" saucer, marked with gold MIOJ; tiny cup and saucer, marked with rectangle in circle.*

Sets of porcelain furniture were sold in the stores. It is debatable whether or not these were intended to be playthings or decorative items since they were so fragile.

Both celluloid and tin sometimes were combined in the same toy.

A collection of miniature porcelain furniture. **Top row**: *Piano with removable lid, 1½" H.; footstool, 1½" H.; chair, 2¼" H.; dresser with removable lid, 1½" H. and 2" wide;* **Middle row**: *Two chairs, 3" H.; stool, 1½" H., dresser with removable lid, 1⅞" H. and 2½" W., piano with removable lid, 1⅞" H.* **Bottom row**: *A boxed set of furniture in the original wrapping consisting of a dresser, piano and two chairs. Box stamped on bottom in purple.*

This 8½" H. black dancer stands at the corner of Lenox Ave. and 125 St. The body is celluloid and the legs are tin. It is marked MIOJ on the sidewalk on the back of the stand. Another one exists showing the same figure standing at the corner of Hollywood and Vine. Art Gill collection.

The Circus Tricycle is one of the more common OJ windup toys. The 4" H. celluloid boy has movable arms and is embossed MIOJ on his back. The metal cycle with wooden wheels is incised on the bottom and measures 2⅝" H. to the handlebars. It is 4" W. The box is marked MIOJ across the right hand lower corner of the decal. The windup celluloid kitten chases the ball when woundup. It is 2½" H. and 4¾" long. The box is not marked. The embossed mark on the right haunch is very faint and hard to find, but it's there!

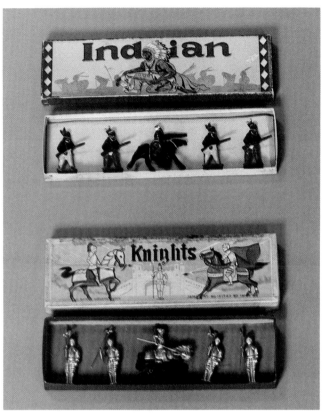

Lead soldiers, knights and Indians are generally unmarked or only marked Japan, so it is necessary to discover them in their original marked boxes.

Plush animals sometimes are discovered in good condition, but there are some out there with worn spots.

These two boxes of lead figures are a departure from the usual lead soldiers. The Indians are 2⅜" H. in a box which measures 10⅞" x 3". MIOJ appears in the lower left hand corner of the cover as well as on the paper liner to which the Indians are attached. The Indians are marked Japan across their backs. Anthony Marsella collection. The box of Knights ready to do battle has lost its paper liner and they are loose within the box and the horse has lost one leg. The box is 10⅜" x 3¼" and the standing Knights measure 2⅜" in height. The Knight seated on his horse is 3" H. The box is marked in the lower left hand corner of the cover also and the Knights are marked Japan across their backs.

The windup donkey has a black paper sticker with a white edge. The black fuzzy dog is 4" long and 3¼" H. and squeeks when you push his legs together. Margaret Bolbat collection.

Wooden puzzles were popular. Finding them intact with all their pieces is exciting since it was so easy for some of the parts to become lost.

After the birthday party was over, the cake decorations probably ended up in the birthday child's toy box. Since they are constructed of bisque, it would not be surprising to find that the only ones available now are unused and MIB.

A toy outboard motor is out of the ordinary. Other unusual pieces include a gun and bullets in which the remains of a Pabst Blue Ribbon beer can were used in the construction of the gun.

This wooden tank puzzle measures 5¼" x 2⅛". It is stamped MIOJ in purple. Margaret Bolbat collection.

Two very nicely crafted wooden puzzles. These are hard to find intact since it was so easy for a piece to become lost. The gateway to a pagoda on the left measures 3¾" H. and 4½" W. The ship is 2½" H. and 6" W. They are both stamped MIOJ on the bottom. Art Gill collection.

This 12-piece set of circus cake decorations is included in the toy category since it is probable that the birthday child played with it following the party. This set was discovered in a bakery along with some others several years ago. The set includes a horse with a rider, a 2" H. standing clown in a yellow suit with his hands in his pockets, a monkey atop a green ball, a clown seated on a pig, a lion and a tiger, a pony atop a blue drum, a bear riding a bicycle, the ringmaster, an elephant with his two front feet on a red ball, a giraffe and a black dog begging. The pieces are still attached to the pink paper liner which is stamped MIJ on the lower right corner. The bisque pieces are incised Japan. The box is marked MIOJ across the bottom of the 6¾" x 5⅜" decal glued to the front picturing the contents.

A toy outboard motor. MIOJ incised under top of the motor. Plate on back reads: IMP SPECIAL TYPE—OUTBOARD MOTOR FOR INTER-NATIONAL MODELS, INC. Art Gill collection.

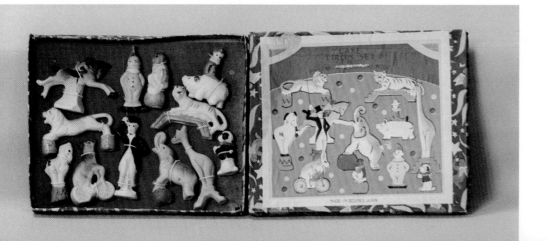

A toy gun with a wooden handle and metal trim and barrel. Inside the barrel is lettering that leads the owner to believe that it was made from a recycled Pabst Blue Ribbon beer can. Almost scratched off is the word "Blue"; not scratched off is the word "Ribbon". The 11" long gun shoots the 1⅝" long bullets a distance of 30 or so feet, although not very accurately. Frank Travis collection.

A closeup shot shows the markings on the toy gun shown above. Inside you can plainly see the word "Ribbon". The MIOJ mark appears on the metal strip running down the right side of the photo. Frank Travis collection.

Many dolls made of bisque and celluloid were shipped for little girls' play. They were quite easily broken and are hard to find since doll collectors snap them up.

Usually dolls in Japanese costumes were not intended to be playthings. Geisha girls were and still are exported to this country and brought back as souvenirs by tourists but they were meant for display only.

A 7" H. standing bisque doll with a red molded tam. This doll, along with the one pictured on next page, apear in an ad in the Marion Klamkin book "Made in Occupied Japan: A Collector's Guide" on page 161 and sold for $14.40 a gross wholesale. Since a gross is an aggregate of 12 dozen things, this equates to 10 cents apiece! Frank Travis collection.

A collection of bisque dolls. The doll on the left is a tall 9½".
Encised MADA (sic) in Occupied Japan. The five 2½" H. dolls in a
box are all incised Japan on their backs. They are numbered 1-5.
There are four girls and a boy holding a sailboat. The box is
stamped with a green MIOJ. The 1920s 3½" doll has molded
blonde hair and is incised OJ on her back. The seated 3" H. nude
baby doll is stamped MIOJ on the back. The 3" H. girl with movable
arms is incised MIOJ on its back.

A 6" H. wind up celluloid doll with grass skirt portrays a South Sea
native. Frank Travis collection.

A bisque 3¼" H. standing doll with red shorts and suspenders. She
has movable arms and is incised MIOJ on the back. Frank Travis
collection.

The *hina matauri* dolls are used in a yearly Japanese doll ceremony. On the third day of the third month (March 3), the Japanese traditionally hold a doll festival featuring these *hina matauri* dolls. When the feast ends, the dolls and their belongings are packed away in their boxes for another year. These dolls are one of the few items exported to the United States that were not made for American consumption...rather they were sent here to replace the ones lost by the Japanese who were interned in camps during World War II.

The paper label on the bottom of all the hina matauri *dolls pictured below.*

A set of hina matauri *dolls used in the Feast of the Dolls ceremony. Their black bases are 3¾" x 5" and stamped in purple MIOJ. The dolls range from 3½" H. to 6" H. and all have the paper label shown above. The lamp is 8⅝" H. with a paper label. The wooden boxes they came in have the same label as shown on page 5 proclaiming that they also came from the Kyugetsu Dolls Store in Tokyo. The second label reads "No. 12 Zuijin B. Grade."*

Potpourri

The dictionary defines potpourri as a miscellaneous collection. That is what this chapter is. To place each object marked Made in Occupied Japan in a separate category is impossible since there are too few items of the same ilk. Many of these pieces overlap categories, such as celluloid and toys.

License plates, although not marked MIOJ, can certainly be dated from that time and are a rarity that adds interest to the collections.

Another oddity is the Mikky Phone which is an excellent application of Japanese inventiveness. When open, it functions just as any other record player and when closed, it is an exercise in portability. Look for 78 rpm records and sheet music printed in English with the MIOJ mark. It is eerie to hear the American tunes sung in Japanese!

Interesting pair of license plates used in Japan during the occupation. They measure 5¼" x 12" and are an unusual addition to any OJ collection. Art Gill collection.

The red plate attached to the case of this portable record player proclaims it a MIKKY Phone. Art Gill collection.

The MIKKY Phone opens to reveal how the handle and arm collapse for storage. Art Gill collection.

The MIKKY Phone in operation playing a 78 rpm record. Art Gill collection.

This end of the MIKKY Phone case reveals the attached Made in Occupied Japan plate. Closed, the case measures 5½" H. x 4½" w. x 3½" deep. Art Gill collection.

Tools make up a large portion of the exported materials. We find hammers, wrenches and drill sets. A wooden keg which held nails has been found. Farm implements include sickles, foot-operated threshing machines and hoes, both spade type and three-pronged type.

Hardware included door hinges, metal mail slots to be installed in front doors, and sporting goods. Fishing poles and fishing gear including many fish hooks in their original packaging have been found.

This 2" high metal door hinge is a good example of the unusual items to look for in searching for O.J. items. Another unusual piece is a metal letter slot for the door. This piece is marked STEMOR and O.J. Frank Travis collection.

A three-piece drill set with graduated drill bits. The card measures 3½" x 4¾" and is marked on the back. Frank Travis collection.

It's hard to believe that something as fragile as a ping pong ball could survive after nearly 50 years but here's one reading LIGHTNING Japan Occupied followed by a star. It is 1½" in diameter. Art Gill collection.

A stylized donkey holder for a whiskbroom lends credence to a Japanese sense of humor yet is still functional, as are pocketknives, mechanical pencils, and handwarmers.

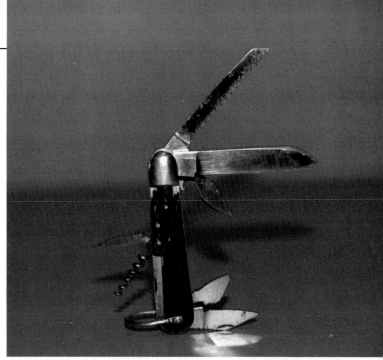

This pocket knife opens up to reveal six blades and a corkscrew. The blade is marked SANKO JAPAN. The brass cap is marked MIOJ. Art Gill collection.

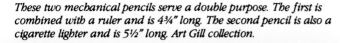

A 9" H. whiskbroom housed in a stylized wooden donkey and decorated in a traditional Mexican style. Frank Travis collection.

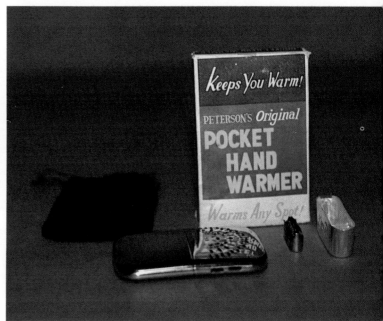

A Peterson's original Pocket Hand Warmer came with an extra wick and a device to pour the oil. It measures 3" x 4¼". The bag, warmer and box are all marked MIOJ. Other handwarmers have surfaced, some of which were sold by Sears, Roebuck and Co. Art Gill collection.

These two mechanical pencils serve a double purpose. The first is combined with a ruler and is 4¾" long. The second pencil is also a cigarette lighter and is 5½" long. Art Gill collection.

Foodstuffs accounted for a large part of the inventory available for export and included the inevitable tea, cans of tuna fish, and the wooden boxes the cans were shipped in.

The SCAP Schedule issued on August 15, 1949 also lists for export canned asparagus, bamboo shoots, cherries, clams, crab meat, jam, marmalade, peaches, pears, peas, and sardines.

Some of the dried foods included abalone, mushrooms, and sharkfins. It is doubtful that all of these were exported to the States but certainly some must have been. Food tins are extremely difficult to find now, since they were bought to be consumed.

An Oriental-looking metal tea caddy. This one came filled with Ming Cha tea and is 4½" H. The wording on the bottom of the tea container reads:

EPI-Curio No. 96
Imported and Distributed Exclusively by
Stephen Leeman Products Company
Teaberryport West Nyack New York
Sole Distributors of
Ming—Treasure Teas of the World
Container only Made in Occupied Japan
Frank Travis collection.

The Japanese ventured into pharmaceuticals and drugs including camphor oil, eucalyptus oil, ginseng, menthol crystals and several other oils.

Clothing manufactured during the Occupation includes men's undershirts, baby dresses, hats, knitted gloves, cotton gloves, and neckties.

These two interesting packets of plaster were sent to me by a member of the O.J. Club who lives in Honolulu. The one on the left measures 3⅝" x 6" and has both Japanese and English directions on it. It is recommended for temporary relief of superficial aches and pains due to strain or exertion. It is to be cut to the proper size, heated and applied to the sore area. Its active ingredients consist of red lead and powdered myrrh. Manufactured by Mori-Rinpei Seiyaku Kabushiki Kaisha in Asai-cho, Aichi-pref, Japan. The Edozakura plaster on the right contains three sheets to be used externally only for temporary relief of headache and toothache. Its active ingredient is peppermint oil. The package measures 3" x 6" with directions on the back in both Japanese and English. It is manufactured by Utsu-Gonuemon Yakubo Co.,Ltd. in Tokyo and distributed by Takaki Sanyo-Doin Honohulu. Both packages are marked MIOJ on the bottom of the fronts.

Forgeries and Fakes

A reproduction is defined as a faithful copy of a form, including workmanship and ornamentation of the original and should not be confused with a counterfeit or a "fake." Reproductions of OJ pieces have been reported.

In the past, there have come to light many instances where forgery has occurred. I know of three bisque children figurines which were fakes. I could rub the inked mark off with my finger.

Another club member tells the story of picking up a pair of metal bookends which were incised with the MIOJ mark. A rule of thumb for metal objects is that the mark should be embossed on the metal, not incised.

We Three Warehouse in Virginia has alerted members of The OJ Club to forgeries made in both a white and a black bisque standing doll. The small white doll forgery is easier to identify. The authentic doll is stamped OJ on one foot, while the forgery has the mark incised on her back. The overall body color of the forgery is pink and details are in bright colors. The shoes and ribbon on the real doll are darker. The forgery has long eyelashes and separated lips.

The black doll is a baby doll with movable arms and legs. The authentic one is very dark brown while the forgery is black, usually unclothed and has white, nylon hair instead of brown. The facial details on the forgery are painted very crudely with larger whites in the eyes and bright red lips. You may also determine the age of the doll by observing the bright white plaster of the interior. Both dolls are made of composition, but the authentic one is heavier. Side by side, the difference is apparent but unfortunately you won't have the two dolls together for comparison. When purchasing dolls like these, use caution and only buy from dealers who stand behind their merchandise.

Another material of concern is plastic, a substance which wasn't perfected at the time of the Occupation. Some plastic items of questionable authenticity have the same black stamp consisting of perfect capital letters. Authentic MIOJ stamps did not have even, perfect letters!

Ceil Chandler, in her *Supplement to "Made in Occupied Japan"* published in 1972, tells of forgeries of a 3″ H. bisque bride and groom figurine. The real groom's suit is matte black and has been fired. The forgery is painted black enamel and can almost be removed with a fingernail. She also cites a doll house bathroom set and a child's set of dishes as being forgeries.

In 1984, a cast iron bank clown with outstretched arms was identified with a forged MIOJ mark.

The only advice I can offer is to study all you can and buy from a reputable dealer or fellow collectors. It amazes me that anyone would go to the trouble of faking such small, inconsequential pieces.

Marks

I am often asked whether an unmarked piece, identical to a piece marked MIOJ, can be considered an Occupied Japan collectible. My answer would have to be "no." OJ collectors collect a mark, and if that mark is not present, the piece is not an item they wish to add to their collection.

However, there are exceptions. You will probably never find a set of salt and pepper shakers with tray where all the pieces are marked OJ, or a set of child's dishes where each piece is marked. But if the tray or the box is marked, then most collectors would consider this collectible OJ.

The question arises of whether or not an object, dated during the time of the Occupation, such as a copyright date in a book or a date on a souvenir scarf, would be considered an OJ collectible. So far, this question has not been satisfactorily answered. It remains a personal judgement! In addition to the more often seen Made in Occupied Japan stamp, there are hundreds of marks incorporating the names and logos of both the potters and the importers.

Some time ago, a story circulated that the color of the stamp had bearing on the value of the piece. One collector was told by a dealer that a piece was worth more because it had a red stamp. There is no evidence to substantiate this claim. Marks come in all colors and sometimes identical pieces have differently colored marks.

Although collectors are now aware that some of the pottery stamps, such as Andrea, Moriyama, SKG, and others, indicate better quality pieces, a simple MIOJ is also found on some of the nicer ceramics.

We thank Frank Travis for the photographs of the marks. They give us an opportunity to see some of the marvelous designs of the more distinctive marks. These photos do not in anyway depict the entire spectrum of OJ marks. This is apparent in many of the captions in this book where I have had to describe the mark. You will see marks which do not appear here.

The marks have been numbered from one to 133, and these numbers are used as a guide in the text of this book.

1

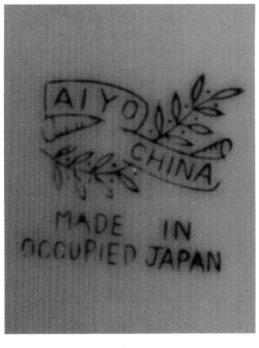

2

3

4

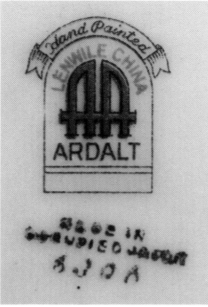

7

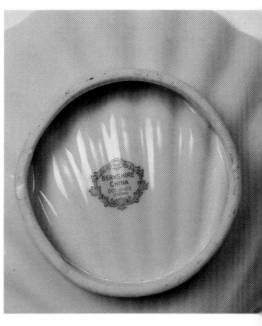

10

5

8

11

6

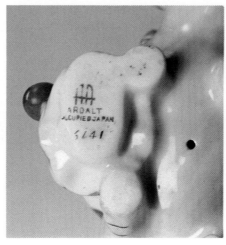

9

12

13

21

25

14

17

22

26

18

27

19

23

15

28

16

16

20

24

29

HADSON
MADE IN
OCCUPIED
JAPAN

30

IRONSTONE WARE
MADE IN
OCCUPIED JAPAN

34

K.R.C.
MADE IN
OCCUPIED
JAPAN

39

LEFTON'S
OCCUPIED
JAPAN

43

HADSON
GUARANTEED
ALL HAND

NO. 12505

APPROX.

SIZE 10 ROUND

QUANTITY 1 DOZ

Made in Occupied Japan.

31

Isco
MADE IN
OCCUPIED JAPAN

35

MADE IN
OCCUPIED
JAPAN
KOUWA

40

TRADE
OCCUPIED JAPAN

44

MADE IN OCCUPIED JAPAN

36

MADE • JAPAN
MG
MADE IN OCCUPIED JAPAN

45

H
Hohutocha
MADE IN
OCCUPIED JAPAN

32

MADE IN
K
OCCUPIED JAPAN

37   38

Hand painted
LEFTON CHINA
TB
MADE IN OCCUPIED JAPAN

42

MEIKO CHINA
MK
OCCUPIED
JAPAN

46   47

AN
Irice
IMPORT
MADE IN OCCUPIED JAPAN
IRVING W. RICE & CO. INC.

33

Hand Painted
K
MADE IN
OCCUPIED JAPAN

KUSUMOTO CHINA
K
MADE IN
OCCUPIED JAPAN
Hand Painted

HAND PAINT
MK
OCCUPIED
JAPAN

48

53

62

49

58

50

54

Kingsley

NARUMI CHINA
OCCUPIED JAPAN

JUPITER

63

MERIT

OCCUPIED JAPAN

55

MONARCH
CHINA

MADE IN OCCUPIED JAPAN

MONTANA ROSE

60

51   52

57

61

Maruyama
MADE IN
OCCUPIED JAPAN

NARUMI CHINA
OCCUPIED JAPAN

HINSDALE

64

Hand Painted
ORION
CHINA
MADE IN
OCCUPIED JAPAN

68

74

Noritaké
MADE IN
OCCUPIED JAPAN

65

"PAULUX"
MADE IN
OCCUPIED JAPAN

69

© 1950 PREVUE PRODUCTS, INC.
MADE IN OCCUPIED JAPAN.

75

"PAULUX"
MADE IN
OCCUPIED
JAPAN

70

R P
MADE IN OCCUPIED
JAPAN

76

NORITAKE CHINA
M
MADE IN
OCCUPIED JAPAN

66

PAULUX
MADE IN
OCCUPIED JAPAN

71

PICO
MADE IN
OCCUPIED
JAPAN

72

ROSSETTI
CHICAGO
U.S.A.
Hand Painted
MADE IN
OCCUPIED JAPAN

77

OHATA CHINA
MADE IN
OCCUPIED JAPAN

67

Pico
Hand Painted
MADE IN
OCCUPIED
JAPAN

73

Spring Violets
ROSSETTI
CHICAGO
U.S.A.
Hand Painted
MADE IN
OCCUPIED JAPAN

78

79

84

89

94

80

90

85

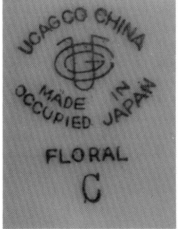

95

91

81

86

92

96

82

87

97

83

88

93

98

99

104

109

113

100

105

110

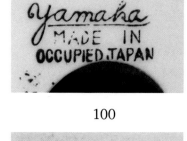

101

106

111

114

102

107

112

115

116

103

108

117

118

124

128

119

129

120

130

133

121

125

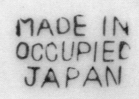

131

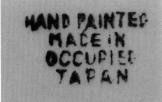

122

126

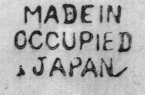

132

123

127

Glossary

Antimony—a tin hard white metal.

Bisque—white, unglazed porcelain, fired once with either no glaze or a very thin one. Usually painted in pastel colors.

Blackamoor—a negro usually dressed in gaudy oriental-type clothing. A popular motif during the Italian Renaissance and revived in the Victorian period.

Capo-Di-Monte—porcelain with applied flowers in high relief employing mythological panels.

Ceramic—a product of baked clay. It may be pottery, porcelain, bisque, earthenware, tile, etc.

Embossed—a raised design produced on a surface by hammering, stamping or molding.

Imari Ware—term used loosely to identify a variety of Japanese porcelain characterized by soft shades of green, blue, yellow and orange-red with typical Japanese design.

Incise—to carve figures, letters or devices into; engrave.

MIB—Mint in box.

MIOJ—Made in Occupied Japan.

MIJ—Made in Japan.

OJ—Occupied Japan.

Porcelain—a hard, vitreous, nonporous pottery made of kaolin (a white clay).

Putto—(Pl. Putti)—a very young boy, somewhat like a wingless cherub or cupid; a popular subject for decoration, painting and sculpture in the Italian Renaissance.

Reticulated—a surface which has been decorated with a latticelike design similar to the meshes of a net.

SCAP—Supreme Commander of the Allied Powers.

Bibliography

Chandler, Ceil. *Supplement to "Made in Occupied Japan."* Houston, TX: Chandler's Discriminating Junk, 1972.

Florence, Gene. *The Collector's Encyclopedia to Occupied Japan Collectibles.* Paducah, KY: Collector Books, 1976. Updated 1990.

———— *The Collector's Encyclopedia to Occupied Japan Collectibles. Second Series.* Paducah, KY: Collector Books, 1979. Updated 1990.

———— *The Collector's Encyclopedia to Occupied Japan Collectibles. Third Series.* Paducah, KY: Collector Books, 1987.

———— *The Collector's Encyclopedia to Occupied Japan Collectibles. Fourth Series.* Paducah, KY: Collector Books, 1990.

Hudgeons, Thomas E. III, Editor. *Official 1983 Price Guide to Hummel Figurines & Plates.* Orlando, FL; The House of Collectibles, Inc., 1982.

Joseph, Marie A. *Occupied Japan Collectibles.* Selfpublished, 1972.

Klamkin, Marian. *Made in Occupied Japan: A Collector's Guide.* New York; Crown Publishers, 1976.

Schiffer, Nancy. *Japanese Porcelain 1800-1950.* West Chester, PA: Schiffer Publishing, Ltd., 1986.

Sieloff, Judie Ludwig. *Collectibles of Occupied Japan.* Des Moines, IA; Wallace-Homestead Book Company, 1978.

Wonsch, Lawrence L. *Hummel Copycats With Values* Lombard, IL; Wallace-Homestead Book Company, 1987.

Value Guide

Availability, finances and desire affect the price a collector is willing to pay. It should be remembered that these values are only the opinions of some collectors and your opinion may differ. Be that as it may, as the market is depleted, prices on Occupied Japan items will continue to escalate.

These observations are based upon my own purchases, the purchases of members of the OJ Club, the opinions of some of the owners, and advertisements that I have come across. They are not written in stone.

Also bear in mind that many pieces made from the same mold differ in quality due to the expertise of the finish work and painting. Porcelain singles (2 1/2"-3 1/2") sell for $5-7 each. Better quality porcelains command higher prices. Pieces with the better pottery logos such as Paulux, Andrea, and Ardalt bring higher prices. This has a lot to do with the fact that the quality is good.

Some porcelain values are:

Page 7	large lady	$35-40
	other ladies	$10-30
Page 8	men	$8-10
Page 9	dancing girls	$8-20
Page 10	ballerinas	$20-40
Page 12	ladies with the dogs	$20
Page 12	Northwest Mounted policeman	$15
	Uncle Sam	$20 (his 6 3/8"
	brother would retail for around $35)	
	hula dancer	$15
Page 13	cowboys and Indians	$8-20
	shelf sitters	$20

Pairs of figurines usually sell for twice the amount of a single. The tall pair on page 14 and the cobalt blue pair on page 17 are valued at $75 a pair. The shepherd and shepherdess on page 18 run between $125 and $175.

Page 20	top pair	$35-45 each
	two lovers	$50
	couple	$50
	musicians	$75
	cardplayers	$125-150
	two ladies and man	$100-125
Page 21	coach	$125-150
	sulky	$125-150
Page 22	porcelain pair	$150
Page 23	inkwell	$75
Page 24	boy with dog	$60
	girl with geese	$40
	seated pair	$75 pair
	man and woman	$50
Page 26	men with monkeys	$15-25
	barber receptacle	$25
Page 27	lady bookends	$30-35
	children bookends	$40-45 pair
	large lady heads	$20-25
	smaller ones	$10-15
Page 28	half doll powder box	$40
	hobo on park bench	$15-20

Large bisque centerpieces and figurines command the highest prices. The centerpiece on the title page was purchased for $200 but I have been offered $400 for it. The knight and his lady on the cover, on the other hand, were purchased at an antique mall for $75. Large (10-12 inches high) bisque singles range from $40-50 while pairs range from $100-175.

Some bisque values would be:

Page 30	sleigh	$150-175
Page 31	angels heads	$50 pair
	angels and dove centerpiece	$100
Page 32	angel artists	$100-125 pair
Page 36	seated bisque couple	$100-125
Page 37	small coaches with two horses	$100-125
	small with four horses	$150-175
	large with four horses	$200-225
Page 40	knight and lady	$175-200
Page 41	large bisque pair	$350
Page 42	pair bisque babies	$60
Page 43	French busts	$75
	large bisque pair	$300-350
Page 45	all pairs	$75-85 pair
Page 48	bust	$150
	tumbled ice skater	$60-65
Page 50	three monkeys	$75 set
Page 51	Madonna busts, large	$75
	small	$50
	Madonna with baby	$125
Page 54	similar pair	$40-45
	pair Oriental busts	$40-50 pair
Page 55	pair	$50-60
	musicians	$8-10 each
Page 56	pair Oriental dancers	$75 pair
Page 57	incense burner	$15-20
	rickshaw	$15-20
	kissing couple	$30-35
Page 58	mirrored pair	$50
	pair of children	$30-40 pair

Sometimes a superior piece of OJ surfaces and the centerpiece on page 59 certainly falls into that category. The owner values it at $500.

Page 60	balloon man and woman	$30-40 pair
	Toby mug	$50
	bulldogs	$25 each
	pair of dogs	$75 pair
Page 61	Wedgwood-like vases	$8-15
	large busts	$150
	smaller busts	$125
Page 63	teapots	$40 50
	sugar and creamers on trays	$35-40
	salt & pepper shakers	$12-15

Most of the Delft-like figurines on page 65 sell for $20-30 each. The large pair would go for $60. Hokutosha marked pieces are becoming more valuable as collectors are discovering that these pieces are usually of exceptional quality.

Page 66	cigarette box	$40
	handled basket	$35-40
Page 67	cups and saucers	$25-40
Page 68	two girls	$50 each

	musicians	$35-40 each
	double musician	$50-60

Children figurines are among the more numerous and easy to find objects marked MIOJ and values vary greatly. This is one area where size is of more importance than any other variable. Single figurines range between $5-20. The brother and sister pair on page 72 value at $50-55 for the pair. The little girls with their big eyes go for $6-8 each. The blacks on page 73 are priced higher because of the current interest in black memorabilia. I would value the shoeshine boy at $35-40 and the farm boy and farm girl at $50-55 for the pair. The shelf sitters shown on pages 74 and 75 would range from $10-25 depending on their sizes and figures. I personally feel that $50 each is a fair price for American Children figurines but there are people who have paid as much as $150 for them while others have found them at flea markets. The Hummel-like children range from $10-40 depending on the number of figures on a base. The child in bed on page 79 is valued at $50-75. The three-figured statuettes on page 80 value at $50-55. In order to value sets, multiply the number of figures in the set by the individual price of each. If a set is complete, it is appropriate to add a couple more dollars to the total.

Page 85	angels	$6-8 each
Page 86	boys with animals	$60 each, $250 set
	angels with donkeys	$60 each, $250 set
Page 87	frogs	$20-25
	clowns	$12-15
	clown riding pig	$85
Page 88	Indian boys	$10-12
	Meissen monkeys	$8-10
	duck musicians	$10-12
	white monkey musicians	$5 each
	Eskimos	$8-10
	brown monkey musicians	$6-8
Page 89	angel shelf sitters	$10-12
	angel musicians	$10-12
Page 90	ruddy cheeked girls	$12-15
	naked girls	$10-12
Page 91	bee Indian condiment set	$25
	bee planter	$20
	4" high bees	$8-10
	smaller bees	$6-8
Page 92	wood carvings	$8-10
	elf planters	$20
	reclining elves	$15-20
Page 93	Dickens characters	$30 each

Prices on decorative plates vary according to the decoration. Some plates marked Chuba come with very heavy gold ornamentation. Many handpainted plates are artist signed, increasing their value.

Page 94	all plates	$75
Page 95	reticulated edged plates	$35-40
Page 96	Satsuma-like plates	$40-50
	square plates	$20
Page 97	coaster set	$65-75
Page 98	larger-portrait plates	$25-35
	smaller ones	$15-25
Page 99	fish design bowl	$20
	lobster dish	$70-75
	butterfly bowls	$15-20 each

Vases and planters run the gamit from the extremely tasteless to the exquisite. The small vases on page 100 vary in price from $2-4. The ones on page 101 are good examples of better quality vases. Satsuma vases range in price from $6-8.

Page 101	powder blue vase	$50
	small dragon vase	$50
	large dragon vase	$60-75
	Kutani vases	$300-400
	pink and maroon vase	$75
Page 103	top three	$6-8
	brown vases	$4-6
Page 104	a range of	$4-8
Page 105	figural vases	$12-15
	green and white vases	$40 pair
	embossed vases	$25-30

There seems to be a dearth of cart planters. Common donkey ones are valued at $8-10 while some of the more unusual bring as much as $15-20. The animal planters on page 107 vary in price from $8-10.

Page 108	top row	$8-10
	Art Deco lady	$15-20
	girl in prayer	$25

Blue and white cups and saucers are valued at $15-20 each, while dinner sets (depending on the number of place settings and serving pieces) range from $175 to $500. Demitasse sets with cups and saucers run between $100 and $150.

Page 110	luncheon set	a bargain at $90!
Page 111	Capo-Di-Monte set	$190
	teapots	$10-20
Page 112	Imari-like sugar and creamer	$60-75
	demitasse cups	$10-15
Page 113	full-sized cups and saucers	$15-20
Page 114	oversized cups	$35-50
Page 115	ornate demitasse set	$150
	leaf dishes	$8-10

There are many different figural handled mugs but they all have about the same value, $20-25 each. Steins are valued at $15-20. The stein on page 117 with the German characters would value at $40.

Page 118	5" high Toby	$20
	King David Toby	$25-30
	Toby with granny glasses	$25-30
	MacArthur Toby	$60-75
	Devil Toby	$35-40
	other Tobies	$20-30
Page 119	dog Toby	$30-35
	animal creamers	$40-50

Miniatures and novelty pieces, including toothpicks and tiny vases, are the ones which non-collectors think of when they hear the words "Made in Occupied Japan." These are the pieces that sold in the dime stores and today are valued between $3-$5. Fish bowl ornaments are valued at $5-20 depending on their size.

Page 124	celluloid miniatures	$12-15
	ivory-like rickshaw	$15
	Art Deco girls	$8-10
Page 125	plush animals	$3-5
	party fan	$4
	artificial flowers	$3
	Japanese lantern	$20

party mask		$12
snowman		$10
Christmas wreath		$4
Santa Claus		$20-25
glass beads		$5

Many of the kitchen wares came in sets and are difficult to find complete. By the time you find all the individual pieces, you may discover that the total cost of all your purchases is high.

Page 126	cottage cheese dish	$40
	beehive honey pot	$20
	jam pot	$15
	chicken casserole	$35-40
	turkey casserole	$50
Page 127	salt and pepper shakers	$12-20
	dinner bell	$25
	egg timer	$25
Page 128	salt and pepper shakers	$12-15
Page 129	multi-pieces salt and peppers	$20-25
Page 130	chrome salt and peppers	$25 set
	glass salt and peppers	$30-50 set
Page 131	stoneware basket	$75
	pottery vases	$30-40

Animals and birds comprise a large portion of the figurines available from the OJ period.

Page 132	two dogs on one base	$25
	dog eating from dish	$20
	reclining dog	$20
	all other dogs	$6-20
Page 133	cat on cushion	$15
	polka dotted cats	$4-6
	teddy bear	$10
	cotton dispenser-pig	$10-12
Page 134	two piggy banks	$20-25
	elephant planters	$12-15
	elephant ashtray set	$20
Page 135	animals	$15 each
	humanoid figures	$15-20
	reclining frogs	$15-20
Page 136	two-figures bisque birds	$100
	smaller birds	$50
	duck planter	$15
	blue base ducks	$7-10
Page 137	large Oriental bird	paid $40
	storks	$8-10
	butterfly	$7-8
	tiny birds	$4-5
	planters	$6-12
Page 138	flamingo	$12-15
	flamingo planters	$15
	salt and pepper shakers	$10-12
	wall pocket	$20-25
	pheasant and mate	$20-25
Page 139	Tomtit and Goldfinch	$25-35

Wall pockets and plaques were manufactured to be used either in a formal living room or dining room setting or in the kitchen.

Page 140	Dutch girl	$20-25
	ceramic girl	$50-60
	bisque three-dimensional pair	$100-125
Page 141	owl wall pocket	$30-35
	children with baskets pocket	$45-50 each

colonial pair		$35-40
fish tile		$12-15
lady pocket		$20-25

Many figurines are relegated to the lamp category because we know or suspect that they were originally manufactured as lamp bases and either have been separated from their findings or were never made into lamps and were sold as figurines.

Page 142	boudoir lamps	$200 pair
	pairs of lamp bases	$125-150 pair
Page 143	Sevres-type lamps	$100-125 pair
	large lamps	$300 pair
Page 144	bisque candlelabras	$125 pair
	blue bonnet lamps	$75 pair
	silver-plated candlesticks	$40-50

Figural bottles are fun to collect and it appears that a variety can be found.

Page 145	all bottles	$25-30
Page 146	skeleton liqueur set	$75
	figural bottles	$25-30
Page 147	perfume bottles	$20-$35
Page 148	cologne bottles	$15-20 each
	dresser set	$40-50

Smoking accessories encompass all the categories of collecting OJ including metal, ceramic and wood.

Page 149	cigarette boxes	$15-20
	ceramic lighter	$15-20
	ashtrays	$5-8
Page 150	Toby lighters	$35-40
	elf ashtray	$15-20
	duck ashtray	$15-20
Page 151	figural ashtrays	$40 each
	Guckenheimer ashtray	$100
	metal lighters	$15-50
	camera	$25-30 without box, $50 with box
Page 152	all lighters	$20-40
	smoking sets	$25-30

Baskets are difficult to obtain since many of them had paper labels.

Page 154	sewing basket	$35
	flower basket	$35
	fishing creel	$50-60
	tiered sewing basket	$45-50

Celluloid pieces bring high prices since they were vulnerable to breakage.

Page 156	carnival dolls	$50-75
	policeman	$30
	other dolls	$25-30
Page 157	dolls	$50-60
	swans	$15-25
	Indian in canoe	$20
Page 158	reindeer	$10-50
	large doll	$20
	animals	$10-15
	small doll	$12
	baby rattle	$25-30
Page 159	animal nodders	$50-60
	seated babies	$40-50
Page 160	football players	$15-25
	baseball player	$15-25

Page 161	bears	$15-40
	Roly-Poly dolls	$35-50
	dolls	$20-50

In addition to the clocks pictured in the book, there are several ceramic clocks whose works were placed after the cases were imported into the USA.

Page 162	birdcage clock	$200-225
Page 163	cuckoo clock	$400-500
	owl clock	$250

The Betty Boop clock is impossible to price. I have seen it priced as high as $1400 but feel that is a ridiculous price. I paid $350 but have been offered much more. Perhaps the fact that it overlaps into another collectible (the Betty Boop) is what makes it so desirable. Metal objects abound but it is unusual to find the finish in good condition.

Page 164	ship's wheel ashtray	$15-25
	Empire State Building ashtray	$15-25
Page 165	horse statues	$10-25
	piano music box	$25-30
	cigarette box	$45-50
Page 166	money box	$65-75
	pencils	$25
	bookends	$65-70
Page 167	vase	$15-20
	picture frame	$50
	pagoda picture frame	$50-60
	small picture frame	$25-30
Page 168	cocktail shaker	$25
	shot glasses and egg	$25
	Seven Gods of Good Luck	$125 set
	key	$50

Wooden and papier maché objects are in short supply. Most of the papier maché plates used for food service were damaged and it is difficult to find them in perfect condition.

Page 169	doll's dresser	$50
	rickshaw	$12-15
	cigarette dispenser	paid $75
	chopsticks	$25
	noisemaker	$20
	letter openers	$10 each
	salad fork and spoon	$20 set
Page 170	wooden apple	$10-12
	rolling pin	$20
	papier maché plates	$5-10

As they do today, the Japanese manufactured a great deal of cameras and equipment.

Page 171	full-sized cameras	$100-300
	miniature cameras	$45-75
Page 172	microscope	$75-80
	binoculars	$50-65

Lacquerware is valued highly because of its beauty. The fact that people were afraid to use it has resulted in a great deal being found in pristine condition.

Page 173	compote	$65-75
	console set	$50-65
Page 174	bowl	$45-50
	covered bowl	$35
	tumblers	$15-20
	cardholder	$25
	cup and saucer set	$150-175
Page 175	wall pocket	$50
	basket	$45

| | lazy susan | $7S |
| | salad bowl set | $35-40 |

In addition to the usual sewing notions, the Japanese flooded the American market with many different makes of sewing machines.

Page 176	cabinet sewing machine	$150-200
	portable sewing machine	$75-100
	large needle packets	$4-5
Page 177	sewing kits	$10-12
	small needle packets	$2-3
	celluloid pig tape measure	$20

Not much jewelry has survived since most of it was marked with paper labels which were removed when worn.

Page 178	boxed jewelry set	$100
	necklace	$30
	expansion bracelets	$30
Page 179	cowboy boot pins	$15-20
	celluloid pins	$10-12

Scarves are a part of some collections and most are marked with sewn-in labels. They are valued at $50-75. Fans come in both paper and fabric. Many are handpainted. The silk fan on page 180 is valued at $35-40 and the paper one at $25.

The prices on toys and dolls are sky high. Part of this is attributed to the spiraling auction prices on toys by those who collect them, no matter what the mark. Also, toys were manufactured to be played with and received some harsh treatment at the hands of children. In spite of this, many survived and it is an added plus to find the original box (you can add about $10 to the price).

Page 181	wristwatches	$20
	Gentleman frog	$50-60
	dime store toys	$15-25
	rubber toys	$12-20
Page 182	doll dish sets	$30-50
	miniature furniture sets w/box	$30
	black dancer	$250
Page 183	circus tricycle	$55-60
	cat with ball	$45-50
	boxed Indians	$100
	boxed knights	$100
	windup donkey	$50-60
	fuzzy dog	$45-50
Page 184	wooden puzzles	$30-50
	cake decorations	$40-50
Page 185	toy gun	$40-50
	large doll	$50
Page 186	dolls in box	$35-40
	small dolls	$20
	South Seas doll	$50
Page 187	*hina matauri* dolls	$100-125 each
Page 188	license plate	$150
	Mikky Phone	$500
Page 189	drill bits	$8-10
	door hinge	$15
	ping pong ball	$25
Page 190	whisk broom	$15
	pocket knife	$75
	pocket warmer	$15-20
	ruler pencil	$30
	lighter pencil	$40
Page 191	tea caddy	$30-40
	plasters	$20 each

INDEX

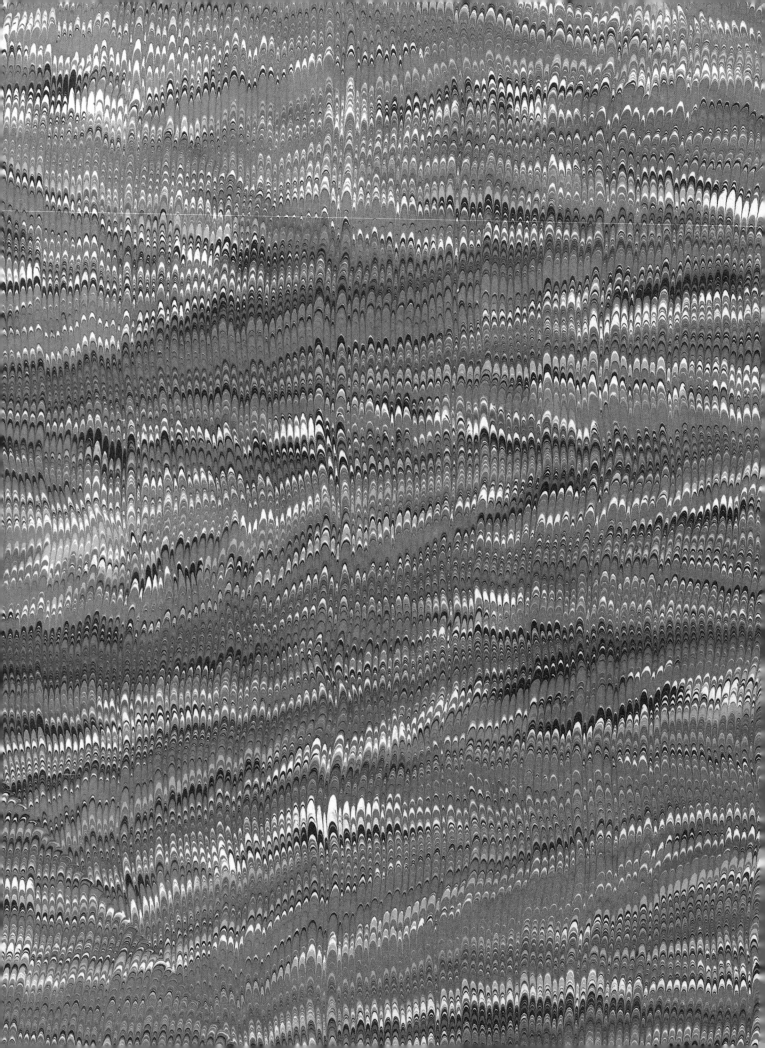